The Passionate Bride

The Passionate Bride

—— The Church in Ephesians ——

Alan Davey
AND
Elizabeth Davey

WIPF & STOCK · Eugene, Oregon

THE PASSIONATE BRIDE
The Church in Ephesians

Copyright © 2019 Alan Davey and Elizabeth Davey. All rights reserved. Except for brief quotations in critical publications or reviews, no part of this book may be reproduced in any manner without prior written permission from the publisher. Write: Permissions, Wipf and Stock Publishers, 199 W. 8th Ave., Suite 3, Eugene, OR 97401.

Wipf & Stock
An Imprint of Wipf and Stock Publishers
199 W. 8th Ave., Suite 3
Eugene, OR 97401

www.wipfandstock.com

PAPERBACK ISBN: 978-1-5326-4347-7
HARDCOVER ISBN: 978-1-5326-4348-4
EBOOK ISBN: 978-1-5326-4349-1

"The Man Watching" and "All of you undisturbed cities" from *Selected Poems of Rainer Maria Rilke*, a translation from the German and commentary by Robert Bly. Copyright © 1981 by Robert Bly. Reprinted by permission of HarperCollins Publishers.

"Continued Story" from *Always Now, The Collected Poems*, vol. 1, by Margaret Avison. Copyright © 2003. Published by the Porcupine's Quill, Erin, Ontario. Used by permission.

Scripture quotations from the New Revised Standard Version, copyright © 1989 by the Division of Christian Education of the National Council of the Churches of Christ in the U.S.A. Used by permission.

Manufactured in the U.S.A.

Dedication

We have had the privilege of pastoring in two churches over our ministry together: Royal York Baptist Church and Weston Park Baptist Church. Interestingly, both communities are located in the western part of the great city of Toronto—the first in a quiet suburban area and the second in a densely packed strip of high-rises along the Humber River. Both churches have been a pleasure to serve. The people have praised God joyfully and received the spoken word with enthusiasm and zeal. We have learned and benefitted much from these faith communities, appreciating the patience and support offered through these spiritual lighthouses. We dedicate these reflections on the church of God to these beloved communities who have demonstrated a heartfelt ardor for Jesus. They have lived out the passion of which we write.

Contents

Abbreviations | viii
Preface | ix

1　Abba's Dream | 1
2　An Endless Journey | 15
3　The Creative Life | 27
4　The Goal Is Peace | 39
5　The Spirituality of Mystery | 54
6　Crazy Love | 69
7　Grown Up Christians | 81
8　Embracing the True Self | 96
9　A Transformative Journey | 110
10　The Bride of Christ | 123
11　Our Shadow Side | 138
12　Going Deeper | 154
　　Afterword | 164

Bibliography | 169

Abbreviations

ABD *Anchor Bible Dictionary*, edited by David Noel Freedman et al., 6 vols (New York: Doubleday, 1992)

NIDNTT *New International Dictionary of New Testament Theology*, edited by Colin Brown, 3 vols. (Grand Rapids: Zondervan, 1978)

TDNT *Theological Dictionary of the New Testament*, edited by Gerhard Kittel, translated by Geoffrey W. Bromiley, 10 vols. (Grand Rapids: Eerdmans, 1964)

Preface

Fifteen years ago, I was asked to design a "sending out" course based on the book of Ephesians for students finishing up a master's degree in theological studies at Tyndale Theological Seminary. Having completed a range of courses over their years at seminary, students had one final opportunity for synthesis and reflection in preparation for next steps within their vocational journeys. In our close reading of the text together, we would unpack St. Paul's thesis that the church is the prime instrument for God's work in the world. We would explore the way this letter to the Ephesians energizes today's church for service, worship, mission, and spiritual formation. We would see the message of Ephesians speaking cogently to the faith community to face the challenges of being a light for Jesus within a secular society.

As I have immersed myself in this letter, working through Ephesians with various groups of students some fifteen times, I have come to resonate with and embrace Paul's passion for the church and its "living stones," as St. Peter names the individuals who make up Christ's spiritual house (1 Pet 2:5). When we enter into new life in Christ, we do so not only as individuals, but as part of a great people known as *laos*, "the church of God . . . obtained with the blood of his own son" (Acts 20:28). Understanding and affirming the corporate nature of the faith journey is of critical importance. We do not walk alone. Indeed, we cannot manage the journey as solitaires. We do not have the strength or fortitude to persevere; inevitably, we are overcome by life's vicissitudes. It is imperative that we participate in the church (*ecclesia*) as the body of Christ so that we are enlivened by the spiritual gifts of "the household of God" (Eph 2:19). Not only does the community sustain us; it energizes us through its passionate love for her leader and Savior. This relationship between the church and the triune God is to be a lively, enduring love empowered by the Holy Spirit. As Jesus loves us, we are invited to love him, and we do this best as a community of faith who walk and serve together in love and compassion. Therefore, it matters to me that my students going out into ministry appreciate their sacred calling to build up the church. It matters to me that my own pastoral ministry reflects this commitment. It matters to me that individuals in my sphere of influence imbibe my desire.

In Ephesians, Paul identifies the church, as John Stott has noted, as God's new society, bringing people together from all ethnicities, transcending loyalties to country and political persuasion, indeed, becoming a new humanity which parallels the unity and creativity of the Creator God.[1] As the apostle describes this new community, he employs the amazing metaphor of the church as the bride of Christ and by it establishes a dynamic paradigm of love between Christ and his church (5:29–32). This new community is given a mandate to partner with the triune God in the work of establishing his kingdom. As the apostle writes, "the church . . . is his body, the fullness of him who fills all in all" (1:22–23). For Paul, the church is not an option that a believer can choose or disregard; it is not simply an institution that exists for its own preservation or a service society offering skills in personal development. Rather, the church is understood to be the body of Christ, representing Jesus in such a way that it becomes a light, drawing people to the immense love of God. If we disassociate ourselves from Christ's church we enervate our own spiritual condition and diminish our contribution to the ongoing work of Jesus on planet Earth. For this reason, our participation in the body of Christ matters. It is not an informed response to bail on the church because we experience it to be boring or irrelevant. How we feel is not the point; rather, we have a responsibility to enliven the church, so that it regains its position as the enthusiastic, dynamic people that God intends it to be.

It is upon these fundamental convictions that this book takes shape. First, we offer a reading of Ephesians, just as I engaged my seminary students, with the hope of providing insight into the biblical text and inspiration to a new generation to take up the mantle of studying, interpreting, preaching, and living by the word of God. We also hope that pastors are encouraged to turn to the biblical narrative, allowing it to shine forth so that people have the opportunity to grow in their understanding and practice of God's word.

Second, we emphasize the pivotal role that the church plays in the *Missio Dei*, the kingdom work of God. The church is ordained to be the body of Christ on planet Earth; thus, it is essential that every follower of

---

1. See Stott, *God's New Society*, 123.

Jesus take up their position as a living stone in the temple of God. It is not enough to simply think about God; rather, we are to get on with the real work of fulfilling his purposes within the body of Christ. We want to capture the requisite energy Paul pictures in his metaphor of the church as the bride of Christ who is ardently in love with her Lord Jesus. As Christ gives his all for the church, so the divine anticipation is that the redeemed of God commit ourselves to the Spirit's movement to draw all people to the Father's love—that we embrace our vocation of being sons and daughters of the Creator of all. Doing so the church will draw on her deepest source of power for living creatively and confidently as the beloved of God. It is our prayer that these reflections on the sacred text will play some part in motivating individuals in desire and practice to become the passionate bride of Christ.

1

Abba's Dream

Ephesians 1:3–14

"Realizing Jesus' vision being dreamed in us is bound to change us. Imagine the dream the Father has for each of us."

Edward Farrell, *Beams of Prayer*

"*Blessed be the God and Father of our Lord Jesus Christ,*
- *who has **blessed us** in Christ **with every spiritual blessing** in the heavenly places,*
- *just as he **chose us** in Christ before the foundation of the world to be holy and blameless before him in love.*
- *He **destined us for adoption** as his children through Jesus Christ,*
    according to the good pleasure of his will,
        to the praise of his glorious grace that he freely bestowed on us in the Beloved.
- *In him **we have redemption** through his blood,*
- *the **forgiveness of our trespasses**, according to the riches of his grace that he lavished on us.*
- *With all wisdom and insight he has **made known to us the mystery of his will**,*
    according to the good pleasure that he set forth in Christ,
    as a plan for the fullness of time,
    to gather up all things in him, things in heaven and things on earth.

- *In Christ we have also **obtained an inheritance**,*
    having been destined according to the purpose of him who accomplishes all things according to his counsel and will,
    so that we, who were the first to set our hope on Christ, might live for the praise of his glory.

- *In him you also,*
    when you had heard the word of truth, the gospel of your salvation,
    and had believed in him,
    *were **marked with the seal of the promised Holy Spirit**;*

- *this is **the pledge of our inheritance** towards redemption as God's own people, to the praise of his glory."*   *(Ephesians 1:3–14)*

It All Starts with the Breath

The Anglo-Catholic writer Evelyn Underhill in the early twentieth century challenges her readers to embrace what she calls "the spiritual life." She sounds surprisingly contemporary when she asserts,

> We mostly spend [our] lives conjugating three verbs: to want, to have, and to do. Craving, clutching, and fussing on the material, political, social, emotional, intellectual—even on the religious—plane, we are kept in perpetual unrest.[1]

Her antidote to our restlessness and dissatisfaction in life—even for Christians, we confess—is to be intentional in cultivating our inner lives. We need to attend to two worlds! We have a double obligation to the seen and the unseen world. While we work at our jobs, build our careers, establish our homes, pursue friendships, keep ourselves physically fit, and involve ourselves in entertainment and recreation—all legitimate and important activities—we have another obligation that supersedes and ultimately outlives these pursuits. How do we nourish our souls? What else do we do, and want, and expect to have? Do we truly long to know and serve Jesus? Or are

---

1. Underhill, *Spiritual Life*, 8–9.

we caught up in the concerns of life that push our spiritual desires to life's margins? What will spiritual intentionality look like?

It all starts with the breath, my fitness instructor explains, as she takes me back to basics for strengthening the core. How do I breathe? The opening section of Ephesians is like that breath. What have we sucked in to the very core of our being—into the ribs of our spiritual life—that infuses us with new energy and passion? As we reflect on God's dream for a vibrant people who share "the eternal now," we are empowered to become more than we can imagine ourselves to be.[2] The opening section of Ephesians reads like a legal document in its density—granted, a little overwhelming in all St. Paul's exuberant declarations, phrase after phrase tumbling out in uninterrupted fashion. But legal documents are not to be dismissed! They contain important information that can determine our destiny—and here, we are talking about eternal consequences. At the outset of his letter, the apostle announces numerous rights and privileges that are ours when we embrace the Christian faith—when we become children of God and a member of his church. If we read too quickly and do not note the fine print, we miss out on blessings that will transform our lives.

A mystical painting *The Sower of the Systems* by the British artist George Frederick Watts presents the Creator casting stars and galaxies into space in euphoric bliss, capturing the divine energy in the birthing of the heavens. Each time I walk by this powerful artistic expression in the Art Gallery of Ontario I am amazed at the passionate source of the divine muse. It triggers the thought that before the universe existed you and I were in the mind of God. We were in the ruminations of Abba before the stardust formed into galaxies or Earth coalesced into its present shape. Indeed, Abba's dream for his people already existed in those primordial days and today we have the opportunity to wake up and embrace it with enthusiasm and intentionality. As members of the people (*laos*) of God, we begin, individually and collectively, the process of rousing a moribund church and embracing God's desire for a dynamic people infused with his passionate love.

Understanding Our Identity Through the Trinity

What is the basis for our identity? What keeps us centered amidst the challenges and trials of life? Is our identity founded on achievements, status,

---

2. See Kelly, *Testament of Devotion*, 65.

connections, money, education, or employment? If so, then we stand on shaky ground as the vicissitudes of life bring many unwanted changes and surprises. High-profile jobs with hefty paychecks slip away during times of downsizing; retirement (planned or unplanned) negates the pillars of self-esteem that we have erected; lack of employment options undercut the career paths for those just starting out. When our identities are based upon such factors, we fall into the cultural mores of competition and comparison, judging success in terms of advantage or disadvantage over others. Consequently, since we are rarely clear winners, we experience increasing levels of stress. When we find ourselves in the unflattering position of middle achievers, we see there are fewer props to support our identity and self-worth, and enthusiasm for life suffers.

If our hearts are open to receive it, the opening blessing of St. Paul's Letter to the Ephesians can transform our faulty view of ourselves. In the blessing the apostle establishes a trinitarian basis for our acceptance and standing before God. The three persons of the Godhead all work together for our salvation and ongoing relationship with the Divine Family. C. S. Lewis, in his important defense and articulation of the Christian faith, *Mere Christianity*, uses a surprising metaphor of a dance to explain the Trinity:

> In Christianity God is not a static thing—not even a person—but a dynamic pulsating activity, a life, almost a kind of drama. Almost, if you will not think me irreverent, a kind of dance. The union between the Father and the Son is such a live concrete thing that this union itself is also a Person . . . What grows out of the joint life of the Father and Son is a real Person, is in fact the Third of the three Persons who are God.[3]

While we puzzle over Lewis' image, we understand where he is going and applaud his conclusion for each of us, leading us back to Paul's pronouncements at the beginning of his Ephesians letter. Lewis explains,

> And now, what does it all matter? It matters more than anything else in the world. The whole dance or drama, or pattern of this three-Personal life is to be played out in each one of us: or (putting it the other way round) each one of us has got to enter that pattern, take his place in that dance.[4]

---

3. Lewis, *Mere Christianity*, 175.
4. Lewis, *Mere Christianity*, 176.

Our status is not based on merit, no matter how strong or weak we reckon our position. Rather, our acceptance is based on the gracious love of a God-who-is-for-us, one who acts compassionately and not capriciously as the gods and goddesses of the Greco-Roman world. It is in this benediction that Paul describes our relationship with Abba and the foundation for our personal identity and self-understanding. "Blessed be the God and Father of our Lord Jesus Christ, who has blessed us in Christ with every spiritual blessing in the heavenly places" (Eph 1:3). We are no longer standing on the side of the dance floor; we have taken our place in the dance! The three-Personal life of the Trinity is at work inside of us.

Paul begins by adoring God for his magnanimous nature in blessing us with the richness of his abundance. He initiates his praise by articulating the Father's primordial choice in "choosing us in Christ before the foundation of the world" (1:4). Such a statement rings with the passion God has for each one of us by affirming that before the stars shone and the planets coalesced we were in the mind of God! Furthermore, the apostle complements this truth by applying the Roman adoption principle whereby a child is welcomed into the family with the full rights of the birth children.[5] Abba adopts us into the Divine Family as his beloved children (1:5)! To be received by the Father as his precious children speaks volumes for our intrinsic worth as the apogee of his creation. The psalmist recognizes our status in exclaiming, "Yet you have made them a little lower than God, and crowned them with glory and honor" (Ps 8:5). We are not to see ourselves as simply one of seven and a half billion people on planet Earth but as unique individuals loved and valued by the Creator of the universe.

The apostle continues his canticle of praise by enumerating the blessings that are ours in the person of his Son. He begins with the redemption we experience through the sacrifice of Christ whereby his shed blood covers our sins and establishes the basis for our forgiveness and total acceptance (Eph 1:7). All of this is based upon God's grace lavished upon us so that we might receive a full inheritance as the sons and daughters of the King (1:11). Nothing is left out of our bequest. There need be no competition or comparison between the children of the Heavenly Sovereign; rather, there is joyous celebration for each daughter and son who turns to Abba. The festive banquet breaks out in song and dance for the lost sheep, the lost coin, and the returned prodigal son (Luke 15). Moreover, Paul furthers his praise by celebrating the impact of the Son on the totality of creation, who

---

5. See Muddiman, *Epistle to the Ephesians*, 68.

reconciles not only individuals but "all . . . things in heaven and things on earth" (Eph 1:10). Through his mysterious work on the cross, the Son redeems both humanity and the cosmos, tying all of creation together as the unifying "theory of everything."

The trinitarian construct is completed as Paul highlights the work of the Holy Spirit on both the believing community and the created order. First, he introduces a personal note, acknowledging that he and other Jewish believers were the first to receive the gracious work of God, "so that we, who were the first to set our hope on Christ, might live for the praise of his glory" (1:12). He follows with the inclusionary comment that "in him you also . . . were marked with the seal of the promised Holy Spirit" (1:13), who serves us as a pledge and designates our full standing as children of God (1:14). It is the Spirit who speaks into our lives and touches us within our daily experience. "You heard," "you believed," and "you were marked" (1:13) by the Holy Spirit, Paul explains to his past and present readers. In the future we will experience full "redemption as God's own people, to the praise of his glory" (1:14). The Father and the Son speak into our contemporary existence, our "now," through the presence of the Holy Spirit. It is the respiration of the *pneuma* which reinforces the "now but not yet" confidence that we have in the Divine Family, which works on our behalf through the expanse of time and unto the fulfillment of the new creation.

God in Solidarity with Us

The triune paradigm reveals a God in solidarity with the human condition who fully identifies with us by walking within the human story. The evangelist John captures this truth as he describes the Son's descending path: "And the Word became flesh and lived among us, and we have seen his glory, the glory as of a father's only son, full of grace and truth (John 1:14). The Synoptic Gospel writers give the details of his birth in Bethlehem, his early years in Nazareth, and his itinerant ministry as an adult in Israel. John announces the same truth in a nutshell by employing the word *skēnoō* ("lived among us"), which literally translates as "to tent, dwell, encamp." John's use of *skēnoō* affirms the foundational truth that Jesus is "the locus of God's presence among men and women on earth" by becoming the incarnation of the divine presence.[6] As we see Jesus, we see the true revelation of the Father within the human family.

6. *TDNT*, 3:811.

Jesus reveals the core nature of the Godhead in his life of compassionate service, miracles, and vicarious death on the cross. As the authors of *Compassion* note,

> The God-with-us is a close God, a God whom we call our refuge, our stronghold, our wisdom, and even, more intimately, our helper, our shepherd, our love. We will never really know God as a compassionate God if we do not understand with our heart and mind that 'he lived among us' (Jn. 1:14).[7]

His entire ministry is about making people well and helping them to enter a space of wholeness, restoration, and shalom with both the Father and their neighbor. As Jesus declares in his first public sermon, his ministry is about "bringing good news to the poor, proclaiming release to the captives, recovery of sight to the blind, and letting the oppressed go free" (Luke 4:18–19). Moreover, Jesus engages this prophetic ministry using what is sometimes referred to as "the left-handed model of power" of questions, parables, modeling, and evocative discourse. As Robert Capon, explains, it is "precisely paradoxical power: power that looks for all the world like weakness, intervention that seems indistinguishable from nonintervention."[8] His approach is not a "power-over model" (or "right-handed power") in which "one lords it over others" through the use of force, deceit, or manipulation. Instead, he demonstrates the embracing characteristics of love, gentleness, patience, and service as articulated in his words, "For the Son of Man came not to be served but to serve, and to give his life a ransom for many" (Mark 10:45).

Jesus is always concerned about the individual and a personal trajectory of maturation, authenticity, and abundance. He does not want us to lose out on life but desires that we experience the full expression of divine love. It is like a rosebud opening from a tight knot of color and possibility and transforming into a blissful expression of beauty, scent, and graceful fragility. So is Jesus' enthusiasm for everyone! He desires that each person gain the realization of the heavenly imagination and bring to fruition the full capacity that the human spirit carries. His is a passion for wholeness, fecundity, and expansive living. Jesus is on our side and gives his all so that we might enter the kingdom of God now and for all time. We are reminded of the saying made popular in the Catholic Worker Movement during the days

---

7. McNeill et al., *Compassion*, 13.
8. Capon, *Kingdom, Grace, Judgment*, 19.

of Dorothy Day, "All the way to heaven is heaven because Jesus is the way."[9] Such a spirit reminds us of the truths announced in Paul's blessing: Abba is a compassionate Father who expresses his solidarity with us throughout the challenges and joys of life; Jesus, his Son, travels beside us in intimate conversation as we make our journey of faith; the Holy Spirit breathes his energizing presence into our lungs with every breath we take.

Receiving Abba's Vocation

When St. Paul comments on our spiritual obligation to "be holy and blameless before him in love" (Eph 1:4) and to "live for the praise of his glory" (1:12), he is identifying what Underhill means to be intentional in cultivating our inner lives. This intentionality becomes our true vocation and our ultimate sense of joy in daily living. It shows up as a strand threading its way through life's seasons, informing our fundamental calling and providing us with purpose and meaning. It is worth noting that the word "vocation" finds its root in the Latin *vocare*, which means "to call," or "to name," leading to the derivative "calling." Vocation does not simply address career choices, as important as they are, but speaks to our personal reality that holds the various aspects of our lives together. This baseline calling invites us to listen attentively to our own lives. No one says it better than Parker Palmer when he writes,

> Before I can tell my life what I want to do with it, I must listen to my life telling me who I am. I must listen for the truths and values at the heart of my own identity, not the standards by which I must live—but the standards by which I cannot help but live if I am living my own life.[10]

God provides such a calling as his voice penetrates and awakens us to life. His call—and our vocation—aligns with Scripture, our spiritual gifts, temperament, personality style, ability, circumstances, and responsibilities, all contributing to the fundamental warp and woof of our lives.[11] As we reflect on these aspects and engage trusted individuals in the process, we come to a better understanding of our true vocation. Alas, we spend an inordinate amount

---

9. Day, *Selected Writings*, 179.

10. P. Palmer, *Let Your Life Speak*, 4–5.

11. See Waltke, *Finding the Will of God*, and Guiness, *The Call* for further aids in understanding one's vocation.

of time planning career moves and financial advancement at the expense of identifying and listening for our true voice. It is a pity that our education system is not much help as its bias leans towards listening to everyone else and not for the interior signals that spring from our own well.

The beauty is that Abba does have a vocation for us to discern which is not onerous or burdensome. In fact, God gives us the energy and strength to carry out the specifics of our true path. Typically, when our journey becomes burdensome, we are filling it with too much of our own ego and pride. If we are feeling overwhelmed, it is an indication that we are either adding extraneous dimensions to our calling or are drifting away from what is essential. Furthermore, God offers each of his children a critical path. Vocation is not the special purview of the clergy or the priesthood but an essential dimension for every follower of Jesus. Cardinal Newman encourages us in this path of discovery:

> God has created me to do some definite service; He has committed some work to me which he has not committed to another . . . I am necessary for His purposes, as necessary in my place as an Archangel is in his . . . I have a part in this great work; I am a link in a chain, a bond of connection between persons. He has not created me for naught. I shall do good, I shall do His work.[12]

Understanding our vocation is instrumental in addressing the fear, numbness, and existential angst that is prevalent in Western society. The daily assault from "spiritual powers" wears us down and impacts our receptivity to the *kairos* moment the Spirit engenders, evoking joy, laughter, and meaningful work. When my adult students journal as a way of listening for God's voice, I am struck by the level of anxiety they carry—fears around the future, security, health, children, and money. Without a doubt the human overcast is formidable, but the lack of understanding concerning our vocation exacerbates the interior turmoil. When we wake up to Abba's calling, his dream shimmers in the light and our lives are filled with meaningful work and satisfying labor tempering the world's vicissitudes. Evelyn Underhill invites us to find our true purpose for existence by aligning our desires with Abba's kingdom, mores, and values, as she enjoins,

> Real advance in the spiritual life, then, means accepting this vocation with all it involves. Not merely turning over pages of an engineering magazine and enjoying the pictures, but putting on overalls and getting on with the job . . . for it means an offering of life to the

12. Breemen, *Glory*, 47.

> Father of Life, to Whom it belongs; a willingness—an eager willingness—to take our small place in the vast operations of His Spirit, instead of trying to run a poky little business on our own.[13]

Later in Ephesians, Paul reminds us "to walk worthy of the vocation to which we have been called" (4:1 KJV), reinforcing the importance of keeping Abba's dream central to our lives. It is essential to stay locked into the vision that bubbles up from the depths so that our vocation is not lost in the busyness of living. The psalmist reminds us that God speaks from "deep to deep" (Ps 42:7) so we need to be listening carefully and follow the Spirit's guidance as we walk life's paths. Frederick Buechner cautions,

> There are all kinds of voices calling you to all different kinds of work, and the problem is to find out which is the voice of God rather than of Society, say, or the Superego, or Self-Interest. By and large a good rule for finding out is this. The kind of work God usually calls you to is the kind of work (a) that you need most to do and (b) that the world most needs to have done . . . The place God calls you to is the place where your deepest gladness and the world's deep hunger meet.[14]

We are invited to keep Abba's dream before us in the everyday and stay true to the Spirit's voice. The triune God who calls us into existence draws us into a place of integration and continues to reveal creative possibilities that impact the world. In a salient parable of the seeds, Jesus teaches that Abba touches our imaginations with seeds of immense potentiality and desires that we nurture them into an abundant harvest (Matt 13:1–9). We have a choice: We can do just the opposite and abandon them to wither and die through neglect, fear, or complacency. Or we can receive and nurture God's gifts so that his dream is realized and our lives are filled with the fullness, presence, and passion of the Divine Family.

Claiming God's Dream

What helps us to embrace Abba's dream? To begin, we must recognize the depth of Abba's acceptance. We carry so much guilt from the past and anxiety for the future that we limit our experience of the Father's love in the present. Yet, St. Paul's blessing here at the beginning of Ephesians reminds us that we

---

13. Underhill, *Spiritual Life*, 46–47.
14. Buechner, *Wishful Thinking*, 95.

have redemption and forgiveness from the past and the promise of a divinely planned inheritance in the future. In one of his other letters, Paul announces his own formula for living: "But this one thing I do: forgetting what lies behind and straining forward to what lies ahead. I press on towards the goal for the prize of the heavenly call of God in Christ Jesus" (Phil 3:13–14). The guilt from the past no longer weighs him down because the saving power of the resurrected Christ enlivens him in the present moment. Similarly, the anxiety of the future is released as we sit with Christ in the present moment listening for the call of God in Christ Jesus.[15] As we release our guilt and anxiety we are able to slowly open up to the waves of God's love that flow over us in the "now." A friend of ours living on Vancouver Island, with her deep fear of earthquakes rumbling up and down the Pacific fault lines, was particularly concerned for her inability to protect her young family during a quake. Thankfully, she experienced God's liberating peace as she imagined Abba's hand resting on her shoulder. Now she is able to carry on in joy and confidence under God's sheltering presence. In a similar manner Abba travels with us! He accepts and affirms that we belong to him. These truths highlight the reality that we are able to give him our fears and anxieties and this is a first step towards experiencing his dream.

Second, the discipline of gratitude moves us towards our realization of Abba's dream. In the Sermon on the Mount we hear Jesus' encouragement to not become anxious concerning the necessities of life as the Father knows and provides for our needs (Matt 6:25–33); indeed, Jesus closes the unit with the consoling words, "Do not be anxious about tomorrow. Sufficient is the day" (6:34). In my own spiritual practice, I begin each morning by listening for Abba's voice, and this verse is one that I repeat as a way of experiencing the peace and tranquility of the Spirit. I turn over in my mind particular phrases—"receive the day," "sufficient is the day," "do not be anxious for today." These repeated prayers calm my spirit and direct me to a place where I am able to receive the gifts and challenges for the coming day. I do not push the timeline beyond the immediate day. I want to receive what is at hand and live out the day in a spirit of gratitude. In these moments I see God's handiwork and appreciate what he is creating in the midst of both calm and troubled waters. This practice helps me to rest in the day as it unfolds, managing what I can and trusting in the Shepherd who walks beside me. It is like breathing nitrox,

---

15. See E. Palmer, *Integrity*, 138.

an enriched air mixture used in the diving world in which inflated oxygen levels facilitate longer and safer dives.

Gratitude expresses the same energizing power of creating an optimistic spirit, better health, and an awareness of Abba's creative possibilities for the present moment. While a negative, complaining spirit enervates the human condition by pulling us beneath a fog of inertia and apathy, gratitude does the opposite. It lifts us above the fog bank and allows our spirits to sing and our faces to smile.

A third practice we can engage for reinforcing Abba's dream is the dynamic of praise. Here in this initial blessing of Ephesians Paul reiterates on three occasions the expressions "to the praise of his glorious grace" (Eph 1:6), "for the praise of his glory" (1:12), and "to the praise of his glory" (1:14). This refrain highlights Abba's restorative work on behalf of humanity. It is seemingly impossible for the apostle to speak of such magnificent truths without engaging in praise! The offering of worship draws us out of ourselves and enables us to see the beauty of the other—in this case, our holy God. It may be the loveliness of our lover or the transcendence of Abba; either way, when we praise, we take our eyes off ourselves and focus on the qualities of the one we love.[16] Praise unlocks the ego's power, which drives us inwards, by reversing the flow and opening us up to the dreams and expansiveness of Abba. As a result, our engagement in thanking Abba for his goodness pays significant dividends in the journey of self-understanding and personal expression.

Gratitude releases the power of the divine to infuse us with his presence. As I am writing, I am enjoying the late fall season of Toronto with magical leaves of yellow, gold, and orange, with a midday sun casting gilded rays of warmth through my church study windows. I pause to give Abba thanks for providing this place to reflect and write about his goodness. This simple offering of praise brings healing to my soul and becomes a touchstone for receiving Abba's dream in my life. The peace, calm, and tranquility of the moment reinforce the truth that I am loved and valued by God and that his vision for me is expanding and eternal. Praising daily is liberating and the end result is a greater inhabitation of joy. As Chesterton reminds us, "Praise [is to be] the permanent pulsation of the soul."[17]

Finally, an essential step towards inhabiting Abba's dream is engaging in compassionate service. The gospels present compassion to be the

---

16. See Lewis, *Reflection on the Psalms*, 80–83.
17. Chesterton, *Orthodoxy*, 159.

centerpiece for Jesus' life as he engages in a ministry of healing the blind, lame, lepers, spiritually bound, or those embedded in destructive societal forces. He is moved by compassion at all levels of his being—literally, "moved in his guts," as the Greek word for compassion, *splangchna*, entails.[18] Hence, as we replicate a life of compassion we come to know Christ better. Paul acknowledges, "I want to know Christ and the power of his resurrection and the sharing of his sufferings becoming like him in his death" (Phil 3:10). Paul's use of the word "sharing," or *koinōnia*, speaks to the experience of gaining a powerful union with Christ through compassionate service. It is not simply suffering for suffering's sake, but recognition that embracing a life of compassion leads one deeper into the heart of the Father's love. As we say yes to compassion, we say yes to the Divine Family taking up residence in our hearts, revealing new dimensions of Abba's dream. Simple steps in implementing a compassionate walk may include the spiritual practice of listening; sending cards, emails, or texts to hurting folk; serving others through volunteering in food banks; giving money for assisting individuals in financial stress; giving time by teaching in Bible school or helping children learn through homework clubs. All of these forms of service touch individuals with God's compassionate love and help to heal our own hurting and fragile souls.

As we say yes to God's dream, a foundational step is taken in the reclaiming of our position as his passionate bride. We no longer settle for simply going to church. We choose now to be a part of his church—active participants in the body of Christ. Enthusiasm for Abba's purposes drives us forward as we are penetrated by his magnanimous aspirations and reveal his infused presence through walking together in faith. We recognize that it is not sufficient to separate our private Christian domain from our public persona. Instead, we choose to make a holistic offering to God in which our commitment is lived out wholeheartedly in every corner of our lives. As we wake up to God's dream we see the infinite possibilities that await us and realize that our dreams form threads of the divine tapestry. When, as a community of faith, we release his indwelling energy, the compounding impact is immeasurable. In such moments we collectively rejoice with the apostle Paul and proclaim, "We can do all things through him who strengthens us!" (Phil 4:13). The church contains the spiritual energy of a nuclear explosion, and when it detonates it releases a fallout of love, mercy, and compassion, bringing healing to the world and drawing nations to the divine presence.

---

18. See McNeill, et al. *Compassion*, 16.

The spiritual seeds lie within us—for many, they are dormant—but when they awaken, "the church as sleeping beauty" will arouse and take its God-ordained place as the new humanity of God.[19]

Questions for Reflection

1. How do you image the dream Abba has for you since the beginning of time? In what ways does this dream fill you with hope or inspiration?

2. Paul encourages us that the triune God is on our side and longs to have an intimate relationship with us. How does this truth empower you amidst the challenges of everyday living?

3. Connected to Abba's dream is the vocation that is central to our life journey. Write down in your journal what you understand your true vocation to comprise. In what ways does it connect or not connect with your work world?

4. As you reflect on Abba's dream, what are the obstacles that hinder the realization of his dream in your journey of faith? Are there steps you can take to counter these hurdles? Write them down and begin to speak with Abba concerning your desire for a greater experience of living his dream.

5. The idea of the church as Christ's passionate bride invites us to seriously consider our role and participation in the body of Christ. In what ways do you minister to others through the church of God? Are there ways that you hold back from participating in it? If so, why is this the case? How can you take steps to re-engage and make a difference in the community of faith?

---

19. See Griffiths, *Shaking the Sleeping Beauty*, title.

2

An Endless Journey

Ephesians 1:15–23

"And let us remember this: God does not offer himself to our finite beings as a thing all complete and ready to be embraced. For us he is eternal discovery and eternal growth."

Teilhard de Chardin, The Divine Milieu

"I have heard of your faith in the Lord Jesus and your love towards all the saints, and for this reason, I do not cease to give thanks for you as I remember you in my prayers.

I pray that the God of our Lord Jesus Christ, the father of glory,
- *may give you **a spirit of wisdom and revelation** as you come to know him,*
- *so that, with the **eyes of your heart enlightened**,*
  - *you may know what is **the hope** to which he has called you,*
  - *what are the **riches of his glorious inheritance** among the saints,*
  - *and what is the **unmeasurable greatness of his power** for us who believe,*
    - *according to the working of his great power.*

God put this power to work in Christ when he raised him from the dead and seated him at his right hand in the heavenly places,
- *far above all rule and authority and power and dominion,*
- *and above every name that is named,*
  - *not only in this age but also in the age to come.*

And he has put all things under his feet and has made him the head over all things for the church, which is his body, the fullness of him who fills all in all."

(Ephesians 1:15–23)

During a recent three-month sabbatical, I embarked on a road trip from Toronto to Tofino, a distance of about five thousand kilometers. I ventured north through Tobermory and Manitoulin Island and along the north shore of Lake Superior to see and walk some marvelous trails, including the petroglyphs of Lake Superior Park and the Sleeping Giant Peninsula at Thunder Bay. From there I traveled northwest to Kenora and the Lake of the Woods environs, which features thousands of islands and waterways, remnants from the Ice Age, before motoring west into the Great Plains to the confluence of the Red and Assiniboine Rivers in downtown Winnipeg. I drove across the prairies, amazed at the vast burgeoning wheat fields while listening to the jazz renderings of Stan Getz and Kenny Burrell and soaking in the big sky country of Manitoba and Saskatchewan. After several days of meditative travel, the flat plains gave way to the rolling hills of Medicine Hat, and I saw the first outlines of the Rocky Mountains on the horizon.

Keen on reaching the Rockies, I passed through the city of Calgary and headed toward the powerful white-capped mountains of Banff and Lake Louise. Nothing could prepare me for the awe-inspiring grandeur of limestone rock faces, ancient glaciers, and alpine lakes, where hiking morphs into a transcendental exercise embracing both beauty and meaning. I reveled for a fortnight traversing the Ice Fields Parkway between Banff, Lake Louise, and Jasper, savoring every moment to appreciate the beauty of God's northern creation. With some regret, I continued my journey west through Roger's Pass cutting across the mountains at Fields and Golden, heading for the destination of Whistler and Blackcomb Mountain. After three days of hiking the environs of the Olympic Village, I paid adieu to the coastal mountains and ventured to the coast, catching a ferry from Horseshoe Bay to sail across the channel to Nanaimo. There I enjoyed a month of hiking in the central and lower Vancouver Island regions before driving to the west coast communities of Ucluelet and Tofino. Much of the time on the extreme west coast was spent walking the twenty-mile golden strand of Long Beach and hiking the west rain forest trails with Elizabeth, our girls and spouses, and the three grandchildren who had arrived from Toronto to enjoy the last leg of the adventure.

Of course, a brief summary of a three-month, five-thousand-kilometer adventure (not counting the five-thousand-kilometer reverse voyage!) does not do justice to traveling the western half of the country of Canada. How can I capture the emotion I felt when I saw a great black bear slowly ramble across a stream bed in the backcountry? Or watch a pod of gray whales frolic a mere fifty meters off the shoreline of Barkley Sound? Or push through the bush to view a towering Sitka spruce one hundred meters tall with a girth of more than five meters, casually marked at the roadside with a "big tree" hand-painted sign!

It was not remarkable as journeys go—others have traveled far greater distances and for much longer periods of time throughout the hinterland of Canada—but meandering across this expansive land was a telling personal adventure. The journey was significant in connecting with a portion of the magnificent landscape of my own country of Canada, but it also spurred reflection spiritually. Again, Underhill's reminder that we have allegiance to two worlds—both the seen and unseen—framed my experience. My extended trip through the rich topography of prairies, mountains, and ocean reminded me of our ultimate voyage as Abba's children—outward, towards infinity—inward, towards the transformation of our souls. This is a never-ending journey and a continual exploration of the mysteries of $zōē$, or eternal life, which Paul describes as a transformation from "one degree of glory to another" (2 Cor 3:18). It is to this great adventure that we turn now as we consider Paul's opening prayer for the Ephesian church, which encompasses the wondrous themes of the wisdom, knowledge, hope, and power of God.

A Doxological Perspective

We learn as much about the one praying as we do about the subject of the prayer in Paul's opening sentence. The apostle frames the prayer by acknowledging that he has heard of the faith and love that characterize the church community (Eph 1:15). He rejoices in their vibrant faith, demonstrated by their love for one another and through their deeds of mercy and generosity. For these reasons, Paul spontaneously reveals his thankful spirit, declaring, "I do not cease to give thanks for you as I remember you in my prayers (1:16). In this affirmation Paul employs the verb *eucharisteō*, or "to give thanks," which interestingly is the source for the word "Eucharist," a term used to designate Holy Communion and the accompanying attitude of thankfulness that emerges when one participates at the Lord's Table. Such an attitude is evident throughout the apostle's writings.

Later in Ephesians, he emphasizes, "giving thanks to God the Father at all times and for everything" (5:20) and "let there be thanksgiving" (5:4). In his First Letter to the Thessalonians, he exhorts his hearers to "give thanks in all circumstances; for this is the will of God in Christ Jesus for you" (1 Thess 5:18). What he models here in the opening prayer, Paul encourages for believers in every age. The apostle wants us to approach life with an attitude of thanksgiving and to maintain a spirit of doxological praise in all that we do or say.[1] Paul's exhortation implies a resistance to a tendency to spiral downwards towards jealousy, grumbling, perfectionism, competition, or comparison. Instead, we want to focus on God's good gifts and to daily give thanks for his constant provision. It is the attitude of the "thanks-giver" that enables us to receive the life of the Spirit.[2]

Thanksgiving is not a naive response to life, but one that recognizes that God is "the Father of lights" (Jas 1:17) and that there is a degree of light in every situation. A thankful spirit enables us to see the truth and goodness that exist amidst life's ambiguities. Thanksgiving recognizes "the presence of the holy"—the "numinous," as Rudolph Otto identifies—in all of life; the Creator's hand is present throughout creation.[3] Thich Nhat Hanh captures this sense of divine presence as he writes, "The mind can go in a thousand directions, but on this beautiful path, I walk in peace. With each step, a gentle wind blows. With each step, a flower blooms."[4] We can learn from the people of the Nuu-chah-nulth First Nation, who live along the Pacific Rim of Vancouver Island and who understand that everything that exists on Earth first exists in the spiritual realm, binding the physical and spiritual domains together.[5] A doxological worldview allows us to live at peace in the present moment, thankfully rejoicing in Abba's presence, raising us to embrace lives of meaning and purpose. The apostle understands this principle of life and gently signals its action in his words of gratitude for the Ephesian Christians.

---

1. "Doxology" is based on the Greek root *doxa*, or "glory," "to give glory."

2. See Postema, *Space for God* on becoming "thanks-givers" and "thanks-giving people" in response to "God the Giver" (p. 73).

3. Otto, *Idea of the Holy*, 10–11.

4. Nhat Hanh, *Peace Is Every Breath*, 128.

5. See the interpretive signs placed along the bog/rainforest walk at Wickaninnish Beach, Pacific Rim National Park.

Going Deeper into Wisdom

As Paul continues praying, he asks for a greater capacity of understanding for the faith community in Ephesus. He prays that "the Father of glory" will give the church "a spirit of wisdom and revelation as you come to know him" (Eph 1:17), a request that includes three different words for knowledge: *sophia*, or "wisdom"; *apokalypuis*, or "revelation"; and *epignōsis*, or "come to know him." Each of these terms has its own nuances. *Sophia* speaks to the type of knowledge demonstrated in wisdom literature where one demonstrates the ability to make good ethical choices.[6] *Apokalypuis* addresses new insight into spiritual matters.[7] *Epignōsis* focuses on knowledge of God or recognition of being known by him.[8] The apostle encourages a spiritual openness to God that embraces these varied dimensions of knowledge by using the evocative phrase "the eyes of your heart enlightened" (1:18). He is praying for synergism between all parties—that God will do something for his readers and they themselves will open their hearts to God's call.

Paul uses the poetical image of "opening the eyes of the heart" to address the need for both our hearts (emotions) and our minds (intellect) to be responsive to God's overtures. The metaphor speaks to the capacity of living in awareness and having insight into spiritual truth that emerges amidst the exigencies of life. The word "enlightened," or *phōtizō*, contains the root of "light," or *phōs*, implying a spiritual breakthrough in our interior person if we are to be receptive to spiritual truth—something God achieves. What Paul is praying for is not about adopting new programs, ideas, or structures, but receiving the life-changing Spirit who invigorates our spiritual vitality. As we open our hearts to God he gifts us with his multifaceted knowledge, leading to a more complete understanding of who he is and what that means for our faith journey. We are no longer spiritual infants eating baby food, but we are maturing—relating to God in an adult way of giving and receiving love. With open eyes we are given a greater understanding into the spiritual realm at the core of the universe.

During our recent time on the west coast of Vancouver Island we spent time viewing the starry night sky overlooking the Pacific Ocean. We recognized the constellations of the Big and Little Dippers, Cassiopeia, Ursa Major, shooting stars, and numerous satellites, including the

---

6. Donelson, *Colossians, Ephesians*, 68.
7. Moule, *Ephesian Studies*, 48.
8. *NIDNTT* 2:392–406.

international space station jetting across the dark sky. Using a derelict telescope positioned in the corner of our lodge as a decoration piece, we even enjoyed a serendipitous viewing of Saturn's rings. Experts tell us that with our physical eyes we are able to see about two thousand stars in the night sky; however, using the Hubble Telescope, astronomers observe more than eighty billion galaxies with one hundred billion stars in each one.[9] The massive numbers of galaxies and stars are always there but our physical eyes are not able to penetrate the vast distances required to view the realities and beauty of space.

Similarly, apart from the Spirit our hearts and minds cannot perceive the reality of the universe's spiritual nature and of our own pneumatic inner space. Paul provides us with an invitation to open up to Abba and cooperate with the Spirit's evocative drawings in our lives. In the Letter to the Galatians he phrases the appeal as "if we live by the Spirit, let us also be guided by the Spirit" (Gal 5:25). In spite of our proclivity to pursue personal agendas, such an invitation rings true. May we hear the gentle and respectful Spirit of God, Paul prays. Like the fledgling church community of Ephesus, may we explore the deeper recesses of God's knowledge and exhibit a fullness of spiritual insight and practice.

The Harbinger of Hope

Walter Brueggemann argues that Western society swings as a pendulum between the poles of arrogance and despair.[10] On the one hand, there is the "power-over model" of arrogance, exhibiting a trust in one's own ability to overcome competing forces. It is commonly based upon an abundance of resources and a position of privilege. Conversely, the attitude of despair, or cultural malaise, emanates from the powerless majority, evoking a spirit of meaninglessness, agitation, and isolation. Alt-right groups express frustration and rage across the international scene, seeking a return to "wonderland"—a return to a time when they think prosperity and homogeneity prevailed. However, the world is changing into a complex, globalized culture in which the answers are not found in the past, but in the future. Chesterton envisions such a forward-looking perspective: "We have said we must be fond of this world, even in order to change it," he writes. "We now add that we must be fond of another world (real or imaginary) in order to

---

9. Dillard, *For the Time Being*, 72–73.
10. See Brueggemann, *Isaiah 40–66*, 20–21.

have something to change it to."[11] Paul embraces this view of the world, as he prays, "so that, you may know what is the hope to which he has called you, what are the riches of his glorious inheritance among the saints" (Eph 1:18), inviting the church to find encouragement in a hopeful future. This hope is real and substantive; it is not merely wishful thinking. It is established upon the fact of the resurrected Christ, who breaks through the death barrier (1:20) and enables us to participate in resurrection life.

This hope is demonstrated in the glorious future that we anticipate in Christ. As Jesus shared with the thief on the cross, "Truly I tell you, today you will be with me in Paradise" (Luke 23:43). Like him, we await our future in the paradise of God. In the first-century context the word "paradise" represented a Persian garden, a scene of beauty, harmony, peace, and joy; and it is to this blessed place that Jesus invited the good thief.[12] It is a place of eternal life encapsulating both endless time and a quality of fullness, abundance, and fecundity. But everlasting life begins in the here and now. Karl Rahner reminds us we are "children of the third day" who embrace "the eternal youthfulness of God."[13] As such we are able to live out our lives in confidence and trust as we celebrate our journey of faith. This present hope, which penetrates all time, funds our movement of restoration and compassion.

Living hopefully and compassionately requires us to "open the eyes of our heart" so that we are ready to embrace the Spirit of wisdom flowing from the Divine Family. We are not to be like Pilate, who stands before the embodiment of truth and light and mutters, "What is truth?" (John 18:38). He refuses the truth as he prefers his own status and the privileges of the Roman court. Jesus offers us "glad tidings" and "good news" and invites us to receive it and enter into the hope of our calling. Spiritual discernment understands the greater riches of our "glorious inheritance," which enables us to say no to the fading accolades of contemporary culture. Viktor Frankl demonstrates in his groundbreaking work with Nazi prisoners of war that those who held on to hope and meaning throughout the incarceration were able to overcome their vicissitudes. Prisoners without hope were overwhelmed by the degrading conditions they encountered in the camps.[14] Similarly, an

---

11. Chesterton, *Orthodoxy*, 105.
12. *ABD*, 154–155.
13 Rahner, *Great Church Year*, 89, 105.
14. Frankl, *Man's Search for Meaning*, 154–59.

awareness of our "third day" status becomes a vast field of energy fueling our decision to passionately and compassionately follow Jesus.

The Empowerment of God

The source of our hope is the immeasurable power that is available to the church of Christ. Paul describes this infusion of strength through a combination of power phrases including, "what is the immeasurable greatness of his power in us" (Eph 1:19), "the working of his great power" (1:19), "God put this power to work in Christ" (1:20), and "far above all rule and authority and power and dominion" (1:21). Through this repetition the writer emphasizes how the might of God becomes the energizing force empowering the church. This use of power words highlights the profound capacity of divine authority. *Dynamis* alludes to "explosive power" as evidenced in the English derivative "dynamite"; *kratos* highlights God's "might"; *energeia* refers to the "operative energy" or "working out" of God's purposes; *ischys* centers on the "strength of God" to work on behalf of his church. As Paul sees it, the power of the triune God surpasses any capacity the Greco-Roman gods might offer the community in Ephesus. He details God's power through multiple descriptors—"immeasurable," "great," "far above"—climaxing the discussion with "all things have been put under the feet," announcing the Lord's supremacy over all creation.

Centuries later St. Patrick lit the paschal fire on the hill of Slane to challenge the power of the High King of Laeghaire. Summoned by the High King, St. Patrick and his companions journeyed to his fortress wearing vestments of white representing the Lord's overarching power. Patrick and his entourage made such an impression upon the king that he was granted the freedom to preach the risen Christ throughout the king's domain.[15] Even as St. Patrick was called and empowered to become a cogent ambassador of Christ to the Emerald Isle, we also are invited to represent the Sender's love, power, and compassion to our hurting world.

The focal point in demonstrating God's power is the resurrection and exaltation of Jesus Christ (Eph 1:20). This event is the critical moment not only in Paul's prayer, but in the entire Letter to the Ephesians, and continues to be so throughout the remainder of the apostle's life. A glorious painting named *Liberation* by Frederick Varley, associated with the Canadian artists

---

15. De Waal, *Celtic Way of Prayer*, 17–18. See also Cahill, *How the Irish Saved Civilization*, 115–19, on legends surrounding St. Patrick.

known as the Group of Seven, hangs in the Art Gallery of Ontario. It depicts the first step of the risen Christ from his burial tomb. On an almost floor-length canvas, the artist employs an impressionistic style using a montage of colors and mystical overtones to portray the risen Christ going forth to redeem the cosmos. Varley powerfully captures the energetic transformation of the risen Christ passing through death and emerging as its conqueror. Teilhard de Chardin in written form complements Varley's visual representation as he describes Christ as "the omega point" holding all of creation together.[16] It is this powerful work in creation and on humanity's behalf that Paul envisages in his Letter to the Colossians as he writes, "For in him all things in heaven and earth were created, things visible and invisible . . . all things have been created through him and for him . . . in him all things hold together" (Col 1:15–17). In a similar manner, the apostle describes the effectual work of God which enables us to follow Christ through the death barrier: "He will transform the body of our humiliation so that it may be conformed to the body of his glory, by the power that also enables him to make all things subject to himself" (Phil 3:21).

Is there a danger of triumphalism when we recognize the hope and power granted to the church through Christ? Certainly this aberration presented itself in the Crusades of the Middle Ages and the history of sequential inquisitions. However, the contemporary church holds an opposing perspective by viewing itself as weak and the world's institutions to be the dominant power brokers. The church sees itself as powerless and helpless before the principalities and powers of our times, resulting in disengagement and marginalization.[17] This view of the world penetrates the faith community so that instead of understanding ourselves to be, in the apostle John's words, "overcomers" (1 John 5:4), we perceive ourselves as irrelevant cultural bystanders. Such a perspective undermines our true identity as Abba's sons and daughters, hindering our role as effective change agents for the kingdom of God.

A helpful corrective would be a restoration of Paul's high view of the church as presented in the conclusion of the prayer, "And he has put all things under his feet and has made him the head over all things for the church, which is his body, the fullness of him who fills all in all" (Eph 1:22–23). Such an elevated view of the *ecclesia*, a key emphasis in Ephesians, is critical for the reclamation of kingdom engagement. The church needs to

---

16. Teilhard de Chardin, *Phenomenon of Man*, 294.

17. See Donelson, *Colossians, Ephesians*, 69.

stop withdrawing and become an active participant in God's work of bringing shalom and restoration to the Earth. The church is not simply a social organization or a service club dabbling in good works, but a living organism revealing God's power through the giftedness of its members. Believing and embracing God's *dynamis* is a critical component for incarnating Christ's presence in the realm of our vocation. Indeed, we are to become a magnetic field, drawing humanity towards God through the attracting power of Christ's love and compassion.

Incarnating Paul's Prayer

In light of this prayer, how do we receive the invitation to enter into an endless exploration with Abba? First, it is important to note that this prayer is initially given to the community of faith at Ephesus. All the words "you" are presented in the second-person plural (Eph 1:15, 16, 17, 18). The focus centers on the entire church body even as it includes a message to the individual believer. The apostle is affirming the truth that we incarnate the presence of Jesus as an enlivened community. The rich Greek word *koinōnia*, often translated as "fellowship," captures the intimate, relational nature of a dynamic community, as individuals "receive and give a share of Jesus." *Koinōnia* calls attention to the nature of the "body of Christ"; the journey of faith is not a solitary path, but one we travel together.[18]

Clearly, if we want to explore the wisdom, hope, and empowerment of God, we do so together as the *ecclesia*! The doxological lifestyle necessitates a communal journey as praise in its deepest sense involves a public proclamation of God's goodness.[19] Together we praise God, and as we do so collectively we encourage one another through words of testimony, even as the psalmists model: "O magnify the Lord with me, and let us exalt his name together" (Ps 34:3); "I have told the glad news of deliverance in the great congregation . . . I have not concealed your steadfast love and your faithfulness from the great congregation" (Ps 40:9–10); "I will pay my vows to the Lord in the presence of all his people" (Ps 116:18).

Second, traveling deeper in the journey of faith includes participation in the benevolent presence of Jesus. As the church body is present within a local neighborhood, the love of God is revealed through its members

---

18. For more on the essential nature of *koinōnia*, or "community," see our work *Abba's Whisper*, 59–61.

19. Westermann, *Praise and Lament in the Psalms*, 106.

bumping shoulders with folk in coffee shops, grocery stores, banks, schools, and on public transit. The values of the church are worked out through the faithful as they interact with people in the exchanges of daily living. An example from our own community takes place each Advent as the church engages in a Christmas food drive. The church family distributes bags to more than five thousand houses in the area around the church. Residents of the neighborhood fill the bags and leave them on their verandas or apartment lobbies for pickup. Church folk gather the food gifts, bringing them to the church where they are sorted, taken to the food bank, and then dispersed in Christmas hampers to the clients of the food bank. The entire process, over twenty-five years, represents the efforts of some two hundred volunteers and is a visible sign to the broader community of the compassion of Jesus. In turn, the local community has responded with interest and cooperation. The effectiveness of the effort is heightened by the visible presence of the church members who live in the area and know the people they are serving. Further, the project is successful when everyone participates: youth gathering parcels from porches; children and parents lifting food items from the gymnasium floor, bringing them to sorting stations where seniors organize pasta, canned vegetables, cereals, and a host of other food into the assigned bins. As a result, a diverse family of believers working together in unison experiences the power of Christ as it manifests the caring heart of Jesus.

Third, Paul's prayer reminds us that we make the spiritual journey both individually and communally. While it is one we share with our brothers and sisters as the church of God, it is also a solitary path that threads its way through our internal and external worlds. The voyage is greater than any other, whether a three-month road trip across Canada or a year-long pilgrimage throughout Europe and Southeast Asia. No matter how elaborate the itinerary or long the passage, such ventures finally end, but our walk with Abba continues from "deep to deep" (Ps 42:7). It is an unceasing exploration of the profound love and wisdom that sustains the universe and characterized by God's compassionate kindness. Such an investigation constantly reveals new dimensions of Abba's love even as an Australian opal displays spontaneous bursts of color while catching the sun's rays. Karl Rahner understands the nature of the spiritual life, resonating with Paul's desires for the church:

> Let us also step forth on the adventurous journey of the heart to God. Let us forget what lies behind us. The whole future lies open

to us. Every possibility of life is still open, because we can still find God, still find more. Nothingness is over and done with for him who runs to meet God, the God whose smallest reality is greater than our boldest illusion, the God who is eternal youth and in whose country there dwells no resignation.[20]

As Paul pens his beautiful prayer, he rejoices in God's goodness, while anticipating the church's response as the passionate bride of Christ. May we share his enthusiasm, drawing long and deep from the well of abundant life, and step forth in the confidence of Abba's guiding hand in our lives.

Questions for Reflection

1. Throughout the early part of his letter we have observed Paul's encouragement to embrace a lifestyle of praise. Identify some specific practical ways that praise can become a dimension of your daily walk with Jesus.

2. Examine your current participation in a local church. How are you contributing to the life of that local congregation? Are there steps you need to take to signal your commitment to the body of Christ?

3. The journey of faith is not meant to be a mere religious experience, but an exciting adventure of going deeper in our walk with the triune God. Daily reading of Scripture will inspire you and help you on that journey. Be intentional in a Bible reading method, using a journal to make notes and raise questions for further reflection.

4. Going forward in hope is essential for maintaining a positive attitude towards life. As you reflect on Paul's prayer write down observations that build hope and bring joy into your life. Meditate on these reflections and give thanks to God for his daily blessings.

5. Paul prays for our empowerment through the indwelling Spirit of Christ. Share with a friend concerning the ways you experience God's power in your every day. Be specific, learn from one another, and check in for mutual support amidst the week's demands.

---

20. Rahner, *Great Church Year*, 105.

3

The Creative Life

Ephesians 2:1–10

"Every human being is born with some sort of gift, an inclination or an instinct that can become a full-blown mastery."

Parker Palmer, The Active Life

"You were dead through the trespasses and sins in which you once lived,
> following the course of this world,
> following the ruler of the power of the air,
>> the spirit that is now at work among those who
>> are disobedient.

All of us once lived among them in the passions of our flesh,
> following the desires of flesh and senses,
> and we were by nature children of wrath, like everyone else.

But God, who is rich in mercy, out of the great love with which he loved us even when we were dead through our trespasses,
> made us alive together with Christ—by grace you have been saved—
> and raised us up with him and seated us with him in the heavenly places in Christ Jesus,
>> so that in the ages to come he might show the immeasurable riches of his grace in kindness towards us in Christ Jesus.

*For by grace you have been saved through faith, and this is not your own doing;
it is the gift of God—not the result of works, so that no one may boast.
For we are what he has made us, created in Christ Jesus for good works,
which God prepared beforehand to be our way of life."*

(Ephesians 2:1–10)

The gospel writer Luke tells a story of Jesus at dinner in the Pharisee Simon's house (Luke 7:36–50). While Jesus is there, a "woman who [is] a sinner" (7:37) brings an alabaster flask of ointment to anoint his feet. Crying and standing behind Jesus, she bathes his feet with her tears, wiping them tenderly with her long, flowing hair, while kissing and anointing them with the costly oil. During this remarkable self-offering, Simon silently critiques Jesus for allowing a woman of questionable background to touch him. Recognizing Simon's judicial attitude, Jesus tells a parable, the story of two debtors—one owing a great sum of five hundred denarii and the other a modest amount of fifty denarii. After a period of time, neither individual is able to repay the outstanding amounts. Surprisingly the creditor forgives them their debts! Jesus asks Simon the salient question, "Which of them will love him more?," to which he correctly answers, "I suppose the one to whom he forgave more."

Jesus draws home the connection. The woman whom you disparage has offered me an exuberant love; you in your resistance have demonstrated none. "Therefore, I tell you, her sins, which were many, have been forgiven; hence she has shown great love. But the one to whom little is forgiven, loves little" (7:47). Drawing the encounter to a close, he turns and encourages the woman with healing words, "Your sins are forgiven" (7:48). The unnamed woman, aware of her spiritual need and demonstrating sacrificial love, receives the gift of forgiveness. She moves from despair to hope, from death to life, from sadness to joy. Simon, on the other hand, remains entrenched in his pharisaical attitudes of judgment, superiority, and pride. He exemplifies the self-satisfied individual whose hands are full, and consequently, is unable to receive anything from the Master.

Which character in the parable do we play? Do we come to Jesus recognizing our need or donning a spirit of critique? If we play the part of Simon the Pharisee, we rest upon our culture's laurels and accolades of wealth, power, skill, and achievement. We are keenly aware of how people view us and live lives based upon their approval. If we choose the perspective of true insight and recognize our need before a holy God, like the woman with the alabaster jar, we are free to act with abandonment regardless of the world's evaluation. When we act from this place of freedom we are able to penetrate our self-made defense mechanisms and discern the life we truly want to live. It is the significance of this fundamental choice that the apostle Paul develops as he continues his reflection upon the journey of faith.

The Road Well Traveled

Paul argues that we begin our life journey preoccupied with personal desires, wants, and felt needs. It is a road that we all travel—"all of us once lived" (Eph 2:3)—before we come into an awareness of God's compassionate love. The controlling principle is a concern for self, even at the expense of everyone else. The apostle employs cryptic language to describe this ego-driven path: "You were once dead through the trespasses and sins in which you once lived, following the course of this world . . . all of us once lived among them in the passions of our flesh, following the desires of flesh and senses" (2:1–3). These "trespasses and sins" (2:1) and "passions of our flesh" (2:3) keep us bound in a place of "alienation from God and from one another caused by misdirected desire," as Anthony Thiselton observes.[1]

Roberta Bondi addresses this human-divine rupture by employing the ancient monastic word "passion," where "its chief characteristic is the perversion of vision and the destruction of love."[2] It follows that the passions—such as avarice, gluttony, impurity, pride, anger, acedia, and vainglory—will block one's relationship with God.[3] Gerald May points out that the passions touch us at a sensation level and evoke the responses of attachment or aversion.[4] St. Paul's description of our emotional state anticipates the observations of these modern interpreters. His phrases "passions of our flesh" (2:3), or "cravings of our sinful nature" (NIV), and "following the desires of flesh and senses" (2:3) point to the powerful impact the senses play upon our choices and behaviors. In attachment, for example, we either long for a sensation, as in lusting after someone or something, or with aversion we are repelled, as manifested in anger. Paul's evaluation of this path

---

1. Thiselton, *Living Paul*, 75.
2. Bondi, *To Love as God Loves*, 58.
3. See Bondi, *To Love as God Loves*, 70–76.
4. May, *Addiction and Grace*, 36–39.

is dramatic: "You were as good as dead!" Perhaps his pronouncement "You were dead through sin" (2:1) opening the discussion could be paraphrased and elaborated: You were living solely on the physical level and unmindful that existence is penetrated with a deeper, spiritual reality! Your journey was characterized by an enmeshment with the world's course (2:2), influence by evil powers (2:2), control by physical passions (2:3), and an insensitivity to the subtle whispers of the holy, creative God (2:3).

We are often unmindful of our sinful behaviors in spite of the sensations we carry. We may agree with societal norms in identifying an action as "wrong" but we do not evaluate it through a spiritual grid. As a result, we do not use the term "sin" to classify the hurtful deed. It is apparent that individuals have been injured by our driven self-focus, but a definitive recognition of sinful behavior is never given. Karl Menninger laments this predicament:

> Is it only that someone may be stupid or sick or criminal—or asleep? Wrong things are being done, we know; tares are being sown in the wheat field at night. But is no one responsible, no one answerable for these acts? Anxiety and depression we all acknowledge, and even vague guilt feelings; but has no one committed any sins?[5]

Such a perspective leads to the mass of humanity self-focused, oblivious to others, with a core desire of personal profit and holding power over others. There is little cognizance of spiritual reality; if there is some awareness of it, it is inconsequential to the onslaught of daily concerns.

Our Western society shares much of the perspective that Paul critiques in our infatuation with materialism, commitment to competition, pursuit of power, and unbridled desire for pleasure. We want more, or "gain" as the writer of Ecclesiastes observes (Eccl 1:3, 2:11)—more of everything—stuff, money, pleasure, influence, travel, knowledge, status. N. T. Wright is blunt in his critique of this craving as "[h]umanity . . . opting to seek life where it is not to be found, which is another way of saying that they are courting their own decay and death. This is to say, with the entire Jewish tradition, that the basic sin is idolatry, the worship of that which is not in fact the living creator God."[6] The other side of the equation is perhaps even more damaging: we desire to live quiet, comfortable, convenient lives in which there is an absence of concern for the well-being of others. A mantra

---

5. Menninger, *Whatever Became of Sin?*, 15.
6. Wright, *Paul*, 35.

echoes throughout the land, "We want to live the American (or Canadian) dream!" Unfortunately, it is characterized by apathy, dismissing any substantive interest in one's neighbor or the global stranger. Either way, such predilections describe the road of getting ahead, which the masses glibly follow, but which Jesus proverbially assigns as "the road is easy that leads to destruction, and there are many who take it" (Matt 7:13).

The Road Less Traveled

On my recent road trip, I spent time hiking on the north shore of Lake Superior. One of the hikes was a solitary experience traveling Pinguisibi, or more commonly named, the Sand River. Following the stunning trail along the high-flowing waters of late spring, I did not encounter one individual on the entire walk. It literally was a narrow path that others were not traveling during the cool, wet days of melting snow. Similarly, the apostle Paul segues from the many following the wide, easy road leading to separation from the divine to the few exploring the path that leads to abundant life achieved by the love and mercy of Abba.

The transition is marked by the phrase "But God" (Eph 2:4)—a God who is characterized by mercy, love (2:4), and grace (2:5), and who acts in a redemptive manner to position us on the path of life. The word "mercy" is a rich word used frequently in the Old Testament writings speaking of God's patient, caring, and forgiving attitudes as demonstrated towards his people. The psalmist offers a cogent example of God's merciful love, blessing the one "who forgives all your iniquity, who heals all your diseases, who redeems your life from the Pit, who crowns you with steadfast love and mercy, who satisfies you with good as long as you live so that your youth is renewed like the eagle's" (Ps 103:3–5). It is a bold movement which portrays God's love erasing our debt and restoring us to a loving relationship.

There is a moving scene in the movie *Schindler's List* speaking to the true nature of power. Schindler attempts to persuade the brutal Nazi camp director Amon Goth, who randomly shoots his prisoners to maintain a spirit of fear in the camp, to treat the prisoners more humanely. Schindler argues that mercy is a greater and more powerful act than that of brutality. The camp director is impressed with Schindler's viewpoint, and for a brief season he attempts to change his ways by granting mercy to the inmates. But he quickly returns to his former practice of creating terror. Goth is curiously attracted to the expression of mercy but cannot sustain the overtures of compassion. His failure contrasts with Abba's unceasing demonstration of compassion and his immense capacity for maintaining mercy towards his children.

Aligned with mercy is Abba's commitment to *agape* love, which is repeated twice in one verse: "out of the great love with which he loved us" (Eph 2:4). God's love is a selfless and sacrificial act, focused wholly on the needs of the other person. As C. S. Lewis notes, "In God there is no hunger that needs to be filled, only plenteousness that desires to give . . . God, who needs nothing, loves into existence wholly superfluous creatures in order that He may love and perfect them."[7] This incredible gift-love is further shown in the action of God's grace. "By grace you have been saved" (Eph 2:5), Paul writes, repeating the word two more times in verses 7 and 8. God's crazy love is revealed through his heartfelt, gracious response which continues to pour out. Collaboratively, the qualities of mercy, love, and grace lead to the terminus of salvation.

Being "saved" is shipwreck language! Throughout my scuba diving career, I have dived many wrecks, including the U-85 and U-352 off the Outer Banks of North Carolina and fresh water wooden barques and schooners off the shores of Tobermory, Ontario. In every case, when the ship went down it was the end for the sailors on board, unless a saving hand was extended. Having experienced shipwreck himself, Paul envisions this type of dramatic rescue as he imagines Abba's saving hand raising us up from the churning waters that otherwise would lead to our demise.[8]

Not only have we been raised from death to life, but we have also been raised to the very heavens, as Paul enjoins through a trilogy of phrases: *syzoōpoieō*, or "made us alive together with Christ"; *synegeireō*, or "raised us up with him"; *sygkathizō*, or "seated us with him in the heavenly places" (Eph 2:5, 6). Each of these verbs begin with the prefix *syn*, "together with," demonstrating Abba's love by placing us in a mystical way with the risen Christ. We view ourselves beneath the human overcast with all its trials and demands, but there is a superior dimension in which we are already raised and receive the benefits of eternal life with Christ. Theologians refer to this reality as "realized eschatology or inaugurated eschatology."[9]

Last, Paul describes Abba's effort on our behalf as a work of "kindness" (2:7), which is another Old Testament description of God's gracious care.

---

7. Lewis, *Four Loves*, 116.
8. 2 Cor 11:25. See also Col 1:13 on God's rescuing action.
9. See Wright, *Paul*, 57.

Jeremiah uses this descriptor as he muses on Abba's love for his people: "I have loved you with an everlasting love; I have drawn you with lovingkindness" (Jer 31:3 NIV). Collectively, God's display of mercy, love, grace, and kindness have the nature of "gift," as Paul emphasizes, "and this is not your own doing; it is the gift of God—not the result of works so that no one may boast" (Eph 2:8–9). There is not one iota of self-effort in this portrait. The entire work of salvation is established on the love, mercy, grace, and kindness that Abba has for his children.

Our part is solely offering a receptive heart engendered through faith. All that is required is, as Henri Nouwen suggests, "opening our hands from the tightness of clenched fists."[10] It is the "fleeting glance" towards God that reveals a spirit of dependence upon him instead of a self-centered trust in our own sufficiency.[11] Ironically, Jesus relates that this incredible adventure with Abba is not highly traveled in his parabolic statement, "Enter through the narrow gate . . . For the gate is narrow and the road is hard that leads to life, and there are few who find it" (Matt 7:13–14). Even though the path leads to abundant life, many prefer the wide, easy road for short-term dividends. These include the accolades of the crowd and rewards established on money, success, power, and pleasure, drawing us towards the immediate temptation of the well-worn path. It takes an insightful and determined response to stay true, and to "keep willing one thing," which is to love and be loved by the triune God.[12]

Created for Good Works

As we "get in the clear with God," as Thielicke so aptly puts it, and find ourselves on the road that leads to life, we wake up to our fundamental purpose.[13] Surprisingly, Paul introduces this calling by returning to the notion of "works," or *erga*, not as a basis for our acceptance before God, but as an invitation to fulfill the "good works which God prepared beforehand to be our way of life" (Eph 2:10).[14] We are identified as God's "work." St. Paul writes, "For we are what he has made us," or *poiēma* (2:10). Other translations are illuminating here: "workmanship" (NIV), "God's work

---

10. See Nouwen, *With Open Hands*, 3–4.
11. See May, *Awakened Heart*, 134.
12. Kierkegaard, *Purity of Heart*, title.
13. Thielicke, *Waiting Father*, 59.
14. See also Col 1:10.

of art" (Jerusalem Bible), "God's handiwork" (New English Bible), "God is our Maker" (Today's English Version), "For God has made us what we are" (Phillips Modern English). All of these translations reflect the reality of God's artistry! He designs, shapes, crafts, and enlivens us with his Spirit with the aim that we will participate in his dream for the world.

In the Art Gallery of Ontario there is a wonderful sculpture by Rodin called *The Thinker*, which captures the reflective person in a meditative gaze. The sculpture is an artistic creation of the human person as the consciousness of the planet. In a similar manner, God's artistic expression is realized when we become his living art, aligning ourselves with his purposes and completing his assigned good works. This truth is highlighted in the concluding phrase of Paul's argument that God prepared these works "beforehand to be our way of life" (Eph 2:10), or literally, "in order that we might walk (live) in them." The invitation is to freely choose a lifestyle that honors God and seeks to advance his love and fulfill his creative purposes for us.

What is the nature of God's good works that we are to fulfill? We must begin by affirming the critical nature of our "fundamental option" for God.[15] Our first "good work" is our response of saying yes to God's overtures of love. It is the response of faith in the midst of a world that by and large rejects faith. Hence, our foundational work is aligning ourselves with God's reconciling action in Jesus Christ, which impacts both humanity and the cosmos. As van Breemen notes, "The great need of today's church is a vital and living faith in God's work."[16] Our work is not primarily about initiating new programs, management models, or innovative paradigms for strategic thinking, but reclaiming the necessity of vital faith that incarnates the truth that "if anyone is in Christ, there is a new creation: everything old has passed away; see, everything has become new!" (2 Cor 5:17). The baseline purpose for our lives is to say yes to God's love. Once we engage at this level, the fundamental story for our existence unfolds.

Paul declares, "We are to walk in the good works that God has prepared," or simply phrased, "we are to live them out" (Eph 2:10). This implies that we understand God's purposes as the Scriptures reveal. We need to be reading, studying, and reflecting on God's Word so that we are able to follow the Spirit's leading. Elsewhere Paul encourages us, "If we live by the Spirit, let us also be guided by the Spirit" (Gal 5:25). As we engage the Scriptures,

---

15. See Rahner, *Practice of Christian Faith*, 114.
16. Breemen, *Called by Name*, 269.

both individually and collectively, we gain the basic framework for faithful discipleship. It is not our prerogative to create a personal template for becoming a disciple of Jesus; rather, we are part of a vast cloud of witnesses who have gone before and shed light on the nature and practice of faith (Heb 12:1). The Spirit shapes and renovates our mind so that we resonate with his longings and are no longer compelled to gratify our selfish desires. Paul reinforces this point in the parallel Epistle to the Colossians:

> So if you have been raised with Christ, seek the things that are above, where Christ is, seated at the right hand of God. Set your minds on things that are above, not on things that are on earth, for you have died, and your life is hidden with Christ in God. When Christ who is your life is revealed, then you also will be revealed with him in glory. (Col 3:1–4)

As we allow the Holy Spirit to shape our minds, the seeds of good works bubble to the surface, and we recognize his voice, which leads us on the fruitful path.

Finding Joy in Creative Living

We are deeply funded in our spiritual journey by knowing that our lives reflect the artistry of Abba. We are his piece of art! He has spent much time, love, and effort in creating and shaping us as his unique masterpieces. Our lives are not mere copies or limited-edition prints; each one of us is an original, signed and delivered by Abba. Such a truth is powerful for establishing a healthy sense of self-esteem. We are the beloved of the Father, cherished children of the Divine Family, daughters and sons of the Lord of the universe. The world may perceive us to be ordinary, but Abba sees us as extraordinary. It is important to fully embrace this reality every day and to affirm it in our daily conversation with God. Further, it is a truth to be proclaimed from the pulpits of our land: "You are children of the Compassionate One." "You are brothers and sisters of the risen Lord." "You are sealed with the presence of the Holy Spirit." We are to rejoice in God's magnanimous outpouring of *agape* which flows unabated throughout the risings and fallings of daily life and not allow the deceiver's deception to instill discouragement. Karl Rahner's enthusiasm is contagious: "More can be made of us than we suspect. If Christ is formed in us, we can never form too high a conception of ourselves. We are more than we can imagine."[17] When we believe we are God's work of art, we foster a verdant environment in which joyful expression becomes the center for our living.

Accompanying that deep joy is a clear sense of meaning and purpose. God has molded us as his "treasure in jars of clay" (2 Cor 4:7 NIV) so that we become instruments which work out his intentions for the kingdom. Through our words and actions the very face of God is seen as we imitate him, living in love as his beloved children (Eph 5:1–2). As we embrace our own giftedness, the divine power that is planted deep within is released through the seed of faith. This results in a life lived with vitality and strength because we understand that our lives intrinsically matter. We have a role to play that no one else duplicates. Parker Palmer boldly suggests,

> Every human being is born with some sort of gift, an inclination or an instinct that can become a full-blown mastery. We may not see our gift for what it is. Having seen it we may choose not to accept the gift and its consequences for our lives. Or, having claimed our gift, we may not be willing to do the hard work necessary to nurture it. But none of these evasions can alter the fact that the gift is ours. Each of us is a master at something, and part of becoming fully alive is to discover and develop our birthright competence.[18]

The choice is ours. We either accept our giftedness with gratitude and purpose, or we bury it in fear or apathy. Clearly, Paul encourages the former response, which leads us into abundant paths and unlocks the possibilities we carry as Abba's children.

As we pursue this path, embracing an expansive vision for life, a surprising spirit of humility follows. It is with humility that the president of the organization or the person on the front line carrying out the leader's directives functions successfully. If we attempt to manipulate our gifts for personal advancement instead of receiving them gratefully from God, as illustrated by the disciples arguing over who will become the greatest in Jesus' kingdom (Mark 10:35–45), then the effectiveness of the gifts is lost and they become irrelevant. Conversely, fecundity occurs when we humbly receive our giftedness, recognizing that we do not merit it, and simply accept the graces that have been given. When we do so the nuclear fusion of the divine-human interface is released and the fruitfulness of a "thirty, sixty and even a hundredfold harvest" is shown (Matt 13:8). Thomas

---

17. Rahner, *Great Church Year*, 63.
18. P. Palmer, *Active Life*, 66.

Merton perceives the powerful miracle that humility creates: "To be truly humble is to be the person you actually are before God . . . It takes heroic humility to be yourself and to be nobody else but the man (woman), or the artist, that God intended you to be."[19] It is the humble person with hands open to receive and release the outpouring of Abba's love who achieves a rich harvest of spiritual fruit.

Abba is a creative God who calls us into the life of abundance. As Jesus announced, "Out of the believer's heart shall flow rivers of living water!" (John 8:39). Our joy is found in claiming our birthright as sons and daughters of the compassionate God, and this includes living in a fruitful manner and completing his good works. It is here where we as the bride of Christ shine as we display the light of Christ in a somber world that needs to discover his love. This unveiling happens in many ways through commonplace actions. We may be a peaceful presence for Abba in a hospital ward; we may seek to raise our children in a way that directs them to God's love; we may go the extra mile in helping a neighbor; we may demonstrate forgiveness in a challenging work environment. Works of mercy in offering assistance to the poor and pursuing justice for the powerless are also beacons of Christ's light. We begin in our immediate context—in our own family, faith community, and work environment—facing the challenges we understand and wait upon the Spirit of God to open up further fields of service in his time. The invitation is to work out our participation in the *Opus Dei* and embrace the path of engagement that the Spirit of God reveals. Then Christ's light shines and the kingdom of God flourishes as we take up our part in the body of Christ. As we do so, we will see the transformation of our ordinary lives into the masterpieces of the triune God.

Questions for Reflection

1. We are all drawn at some level to the road well traveled. What attractions draw you to the wide way that resists Abba's love?

2. The road less traveled centers on love, mercy, grace, and kindness, which as an aggregate presents the true nature of our loving God. Which of these characteristics are central in your faith journey? Why? How? Meditate on these qualities and give thanks for Abba's invitation for experiencing the abundant life.

---

19. R. King, *Thomas Merton and Thich Nhat Hanh*, 49.

3. Our artist God has been shaping you into his work of art. He has also invited you to join the artistic process by filling up the good works he has established on your behalf. In your journal create a mind map which includes the good works you have completed, the ones you are engaging, and those which are emerging. Notice the connections and consider new steps you may take in your creative work for God.

4. Parker Palmer has noted, "Some of the most powerful clues to our true gifts are buried deep in childhood, when we said and did and felt things without censoring them through external values or expectations."[20] As Van Morrison sings in his album *Hymns to the Quiet*, "Go 'way, 'way back" to the creative days of your childhood. Compose a childhood autobiography, detailing joys, pleasures, time spent, aversions, dreams, and hopes as an exercise in revealing your true giftedness. Write your autobiography to see what it reveals in moving you towards new vistas of creativity.

---

20. P. Palmer, *Active Life*, 68.

4

The Goal Is Peace

Ephesians 2:11–22

"One day we must come to see that peace is not merely a distant goal that we seek, but a means by which we arrive at that goal. We must pursue peaceful ends through peaceful means."[1]

Martin Luther King Jr.

"So then, remember that at one time you Gentiles by birth,
> called 'the uncircumcision'—a physical circumcision made in the flesh by human hands—

remember that you were at that time without Christ,
> being aliens from the commonwealth of Israel, and strangers to the covenants of promise,
>
> having no hope and without God in the world.

But now in Christ Jesus you who once were far off have been brought near by the blood of
> Christ.

For he is our peace;

in his flesh he has made both groups into one and has broken down the dividing wall,
> that is, the hostility between us.

He has abolished the law with its commandments and ordinances,

---

1. M. King, *Words of Martin Luther King Jr.*, 83.

THE PASSIONATE BRIDE

so that he might create in himself one new humanity in place of the two,
thus making peace,
and might reconcile both groups to God in one body through the cross thus putting to death that hostility through it.

*So he came and **proclaimed peace to you who were far off and peace to those who were near**;*
    for through him both of us have access in one Spirit to the Father.

So then you are no longer strangers and aliens,
    but you are citizens with the saints and also members of the household of God,
    built upon the foundation of the apostles and prophets,
    with Christ Jesus himself as the cornerstone.

In him the whole structure is joined together and grows into a holy temple in the Lord; in whom you are also built together spiritually into a dwelling-place for God."
(Ephesians 2:11–22)

The Pulitzer Prize play *Fences*, by August Wilson, tells the story of Troy Maxson, his wife, Rose, and their son, Cory, living in the city of Pittsburgh in the 1950s. Troy works as a garbage collector alongside his friend Jim and dwells in a simple house bought by a government payout to his older brother, Gabe, who had sustained a head injury in World War II. Life has been tough on Troy and he feels the weight of it every day. In a former life he played professional baseball in the Negro League but was too old when the color barrier was broken in the Big Leagues. He never accepted this argument, seeing his rejection as an act of prejudice. In his present job he resents standing on the back of the truck picking up waste when the white driver sits comfortably in his cab. The fact that even his house was purchased by a check made out to his brother is a constant reminder of life's disappointments. The powers that be have treated him unfairly. There is little joy and numerous reminders reinforcing his jaded view of self. As an act of defiance Troy decides to build a fence surrounding his backyard to keep his enemies out and to keep in the few people that he loves. The construction of the fence becomes a symbol for self-protection against unseen malevolent forces—including "the Grim Reaper," Death—that align themselves, seeking his destruction. Building the fence is his final desperate act to ward off the devastation of everything he loves and values.

Like Wilson's protagonist, Troy, our world is skilled in the erection of walls and fences. During the historical setting for the play in the 1950s, the division between the West and the Soviet Union was called the Iron Curtain; apartheid policies maintained racial segregation in South Africa; the city of Berlin was split by a wall into east and west. A decade later my own birth city of Belfast was marked by a series of walls—euphemistically called "Peace Walls"— separating Catholics and Protestants along religious lines. In the present context, plans are made to build a wall spanning the entire length of the United States border with Mexico, ostensibly to keep illegal immigrants from crossing into America. Alas, our contemporary society is astute at building walls and less proficient in the establishment of peace. The apostle Paul invites us to reflect on this proclivity for building walls and encourages us instead to embrace the world of peace making.

Living with No Hope

St. Paul encourages the Ephesian believers to remember their pre-conversion days; indeed, he exhorts them twice "to remember"—"to remember again" (Eph 2:11, 12)—their previous spiritual condition. Speaking bluntly, the apostle reminds them that they were "without Christ" and "without God" (2:12). "Without Christ" signifies that they were "without the Messiah," and therefore not part of "the commonwealth of Israel." "Without God"—the word Paul uses is *atheos*, from which we derive "atheist"—does not mean godless, for they believed in the Greco-Roman panoply of gods, but lacked an understanding and relationship to the one true God. The combination of "without Christ" and "without God" reinforces to the faith community their absolute dependence on the grace and compassion of Abba for their participation in the people of God.

Pushing harder, Paul identifies three derivatives of what it means to be "without Christ" and "without God," of which the first is "being aliens from the commonwealth of Israel" (2:12). Paul uses the uncommon word *apallotrioō*, "aliens" or "alienated," twice in this Letter to the Ephesians—here and in chapter 4—in which he argues that the Ephesians were "alienated from the life of God because of their ignorance and hardness of heart"

(4:18). The verb "to alienate" includes the ideas of estrangement, exclusion, and alienation, and here it is linked to "commonwealth" or "citizenship" (*politeia*), which closely resonates with Paul, who held the status of citizenship in both Israel and the Roman Empire.[2] By connecting these two words Paul clarifies for the Ephesians that they were disenfranchised from the rights and benefits of the kingdom of God and were adrift before the Lord of the universe. A second consequence for Paul is that they were *xenoi*, or "strangers to the covenants of promise" (2:12); they were viewed as total outsiders to the pledges given to Israel. Such an identification rings powerfully in our contemporary age where xenophobia and resistance to immigration and the rise of the number of displaced peoples has wreaked havoc in our world. Third, the apostle announces that the Ephesian community had "no hope in the world" (2:12). They were indeed hopeless, as the Greco-Roman gods acted in capricious and self-serving ways, keeping the people in despair and living beneath a fate-directed system. The prevailing ideologies of stoicism ("keep a stiff upper lip amidst the exigencies of life") and epicureanism ("enjoy the pleasures of each day because that is all we have") offered little in the way of substantive hope, leaving people adrift in an ocean of fear and unending anxiety.

Paul's call to remember or look back on one's life from a spiritual perspective is presented in a variety of his writings. In the Letter to the Colossians he also writes, "If with Christ you died to the elemental spirits of the universe, why do you live as if you still belonged to the world?" (Col 2:20).[3] Paul encourages the believers to learn from their past actions and not to blindly return to old patterns of behavior. The writer of 1 Peter mirrors this exhortation as he writes, "You have already spent enough time in doing what the Gentiles like to do, living in licentiousness, passion, drunkenness, revels, carousing, and lawless idolatry" (1 Pet 4:3). They have already pursued the epicurean lifestyle and found it wanting, so it bears no merit to continue along this path. Similarly, there is great value for us to "remember again" where we have come from and to reflect on our tendencies for repeating old behavioral patterns. When aspects of the false self arise, let us ask ourselves whether the old compensations are worth the bondage that our addictions create? Is the payoff worth the lack of freedom? Such reflection slows our entanglement with prior hurtful movements and quickens our spirits for persevering and enjoying the freedom Christ proffers.

2. Stott, *God's New Society*, 90.
3. See also Col 3:7 and Gal 3:1–4.

Christ Is Our Hope and Peace

Paul offers the resolution to the problem of alienation by proclaiming that those who were "far off" have been "brought near" through the sacrifice of the Messiah (Eph 2:13). The spatial language of "far off"/"brought near" mirrors the language of Isaiah as the prophet declares, "Peace, peace, to the far and the near, says the Lord" (Isa 57:19), and also his message describing the Messiah as the Prince of Peace: "How beautiful upon the mountains are the feet of the messenger who announces peace, who brings good news, who announces salvation, who says to Zion, 'Your God reigns'" (Isa 52:7). Paul makes the link explicit as he states, "For he [Christ the Messiah] is our peace" and highlights this connection by using the Greek word *eirēnē*, or "peace," which translates the Hebrew word *shālôm*. The word *shālôm/eirēnē* describes more than an absence of conflict. It includes "[a] sense of general well-being, the source and giver of which is Yahweh alone" and which is manifested through Christ the Messiah.[4] Paul reinforces this truth throughout his writings: "And let the peace of Christ rule in your hearts" (Col 3:15); "Therefore, since we are justified by faith, we have peace with God through our Lord Jesus Christ" (Rom 5:1); and in the context of addressing Christ's salvific work, "For the kingdom of God is not food and drink but righteousness and peace and joy in the Holy Spirit" (Rom 14:17).

For Paul, this peace is accomplished through the breaking down of "the dividing wall, that is, the hostility between us" (Eph 2:14). As Ralph Martin points out, this action of deconstruction alludes to a double reconciliation process that includes a restoration of our relationship with Abba and our relationship with one another.[5] John Muddiman suggests two possibilities for Paul's declaration of the "dividing wall being broken down" (2:14). The phrase may refer to the destruction of the physical wall which separated the Court of Women from the Court of Gentiles in the Jerusalem temple, or metaphorically to the ending of the ceremonial law (*tôrâh*) separating Jews from Gentiles.[6] Muddiman presses further, arguing that the breaking down of the wall of hostility refers to "all the expressions of social enmity, familiar to any Jew or Gentile in the Hellenistic world, the differences in place of residence, manner of worship, food and dress, politics and ethics, and above all the blank wall of mutual incomprehension, fear and contempt

---

4. *NIDNTT*, 2:777, 780.
5. Martin, *Ephesians, Colossians*, 34.
6. Muddiman, *Epistle to the Ephesians*, 128.

between the two groups."⁷ This description accurately reflects Paul's announcement of the holistic liberation accomplished through Christ's work. The denouement of this astounding eradication is the creation of "one new humanity" (Eph 2:15) whereby the Messiah revolutionizes the people of God to include individuals from every nation and ethnicity in the world. It is no longer restricted to the nation of Israel. Built on the promises to Abraham, it extends to peoples of every nation, creating a single new humanity transcending color, status, sex, and any other identifiable division (Gal 3:28; Col 3:11).

Paul reiterates one more time that through Christ's work on the cross the Messiah has proclaimed peace to "you who were far off and peace to those who were near" (2:16–17); through him both groups have "access in one Spirit to the Father" (2:18). In contrast to the perceived limited access to the multiple gods of the Greco-Roman pantheon, through Christ the Ephesian Christians have access to the one true God, superior to any other power imagined or real—including the newest god in town, Caesar! They now have the privilege of going directly to the Father in prayer or praise and are freed from the facsimiles of religious practice offered in the Temple of Artemis. Likewise, we have the opportunity to go to Abba and experience his peace directly if we take advantage of the invitation to meet with him daily.⁸ Unfortunately, we are often slow to act on the graces Abba offers and seem to be satisfied with a distant relationship with the Father. There is a need to acknowledge our spiritual reticence and to guard against our proclivity for fence-building, separating us from God and others. John Stott cautions us to be aware of this tendency, even within the bounds of the new humanity:

> For even in the church there is often alienation, disunity and discord. And Christians erect new barriers in place of the old—now a colour bar, now racism, nationalism or tribalism, now personal animosities engendered by pride, prejudice, jealousy and the unforgiving spirit . . . a denominationalism which turns churches into sects and contradicts the unity and universality of Christ's church.⁹

The divisions that Stott enumerates both mock Christ's work before an unbelieving world and diminish the role the church is able to play within it as an agent of God's peace.

7. Muddiman, *Epistle to the Ephesians*, 128.
8. See Heb 3:7; 13:15; 4:7.
9. Stott, *God's New Society*, 110–11.

The unit ends with the apostle employing three metaphors that describe the access we have attained in Christ.[10] First, believers have access to the Father due to their citizenship in the kingdom of God: "So then you are no longer strangers and aliens, but you are citizens with the saints" (2:19).[11] The word *sympolitēs* he employs for "citizens" counters the previous negation of citizenship when he describes the Ephesians as "aliens from the commonwealth [*politeia*] of Israel" (2:12). The message is one of inclusion, speaking powerfully today against the political movements proclaiming white superiority and rejecting the voices and equal participation of diverse peoples.

Second, not only are the Gentiles equal partners in God's kingdom, but they are children in God's family as acknowledged through the second metaphor "members of the household of God" (2:19).[12] The term "household" or "family" addresses the reality of belonging and of being fully accepted by the Father. In our fractured world there is perhaps no greater need than to feel the *shālôm* of belonging. The holding camps for migrants and the circuitous journeys of displaced peoples around the globe demonstrate this desperate absence of *shālôm*. Our churches have the opportunity to become places of inclusion where individuals receive the love, compassion, and acceptance of Christ rather than the rejection which emanates from fearful nations. Indeed, we are called to become shining lights in a darkened world, where the stranger is received and valued as a person created in God's image. As Paul enjoins later in his letter, "But now in the Lord you are light. Live as children of light—for the fruit of the light is found in all that is good and right and true" (5:8–9).

The third and final metaphor portrays the Gentiles' participation in God's "holy temple" (2: 21), which we imagine resounded powerfully within the faith community of Ephesus, where the Temple to Artemis, one of the seven wonders of the ancient world and known throughout Asia Minor, stood.[13] Here Paul celebrates the truth that God no longer dwells in a physical temple but resides in the new people of God. Indeed, Abba dwells within every believer and together we are shaped into a spiritual temple with each person fitting spiritually into the new dwelling place of God (2:22). In this new temple each stone is valuable and plays an intrinsic role, like individual jewels in a beautiful mosaic. Together the three metaphors—citizens in

---

10. See Cousar, *Letters of Paul*, 173–74, on metaphors for the church.
11. See Stott, *God's New Society*, 104–5.
12. Stott, *God's New Society*, 105–6.
13. Stott, *God's New Society*, 106–10.

God's kingdom, children in God's family, and stones in God's temple—articulate the transformation granted to the Gentiles, who were once alienated but are now wholly reconciled as integral members of God's Third Race. The challenge to the Ephesian church then and the church now as the incipient new humanity is to become the vanguard for peacemaking in a world wrought with turmoil.

Peacemaking within the Church Community

The message of Ephesians is that we experience peace as we enter into a living relationship with the Messiah, Jesus Christ. For Paul, this claim is not simply an idea or a theory but a core truth which leads us forward on a path of emulating the values and lifestyle of the King. If Christ is the Prince of Peace, then we as his followers are called to live lives of peace. Thomas Merton describes this transformational relationship in these daring words: "Christ did not come to bring peace to the world 'as a kind of spiritual tranquilizer'; rather he gave to his disciples 'a vocation and a task, to struggle in the world of violence to establish his peace not only in their own hearts but in society itself.'"[14] The author Robert King complements Merton's voice with the words of Nobel Peace Prize winner Thich Nhat Hanh, "Only by being peace can we hope to make peace in the world."[15] There is no peace if we do not embody it and do the hard work of pursuing peace in our world. Our challenge is to find a way forward which opens up a place of engagement in the process of seeking peace. To this end we find Scott Peck's work in *A World Waiting to Be Born* to be helpful as he cites the definition of prayer from theologian Matthew Fox as "a radical response to the mysteries of life."[16] Peck makes three observations which flow from this definition: first, prayer is a radical response; second, this radical response energizes us to move from reflection to an engagement of action; and third, prayer is a mysterious work directed by the Spirit, who works in an elusive way to achieve the purposes of God. Peacemaking is like prayer. It is a radical response to a disjointed and fractured world.[17] The pursuit of peace is also a mysterious journey and the precise steps are not always clear.

14. R. King, *Thomas Merton and Thich Nhat Hanh*, 60.
15. R. King, *Thomas Merton and Thich Nhat Hanh*, 22.
16. Peck, *World Waiting to Be Born*, 85.
17. Peck, *World Waiting to Be Born*, 85. See also Fox, *On Becoming a Musical Mystical Bear*, 49–116.

The Christian's first arena for engagement in peacemaking is the local church. The writings of Paul and his fellow apostles are replete with the encouragement to love and be at peace with one another. Here in the Ephesians letter he admonishes his listeners "to lead a life worthy of [their] calling . . . with all humility and gentleness, with patience, bearing with one another in love" (Eph 4:1–2); he writes to the Colossian Christians, "Above all, clothe yourselves with love, which binds everything together in perfect harmony" (Col 3:14); to the Corinthians he points out, "If I give away all of my possessions, and if I hand over my body so that I may boast, but do not have love, I gain nothing" (1 Cor 13:3). The apostle John cautions his hearers, "Whoever does not love does not know God, for God is love" (1 John 4:8). Love is the core of knowing and pleasing God because God is love and his love identifies us as his children.

A story dating back to the time of Jerome recounts an event when the faith community gathered to hear from the elderly apostle John. Carried into the assembly, the evangelist spoke the words, "Little children, love one another." When the people asked for a development of his instruction, he simply repeated, "Little children, love one another." Perplexed by the repetition, they queried why he gave no variation on the theme, and he replied, "Because it is the commandment of the Lord, and if it is done, it suffices."[18] John knew that love is the central reality and if we practice it, peace and harmony will be manifested in the community.

The challenge we face is to maintain a loving attitude amidst the frustrations emanating within a fragile community. The church is a messy place due to the emotional baggage, competing opinions, and desire for power naturally prevalent in our faith communities. Cliques often form that create division and hinder a spirit of unity and service within the community. As a result, there is a great need for peacemakers to rise up within the body of Christ to use their spiritual gifts to draw people together. Individuals sometimes move from one church to another whenever tension arises within the congregations rather than remaining to help resolve the issues at hand. Of course, this flight is facilitated by the plethora of choice in North American churches and the prevailing attitude of consumerism, which identifies the "best" church that "meets my needs." Such a combination erodes the necessary commitment for bringing our spiritual gifts together so that God's temple is fittingly constructed (Eph 2:22). Paul's call is for perseverance and a continuation of working together for peace in spite of

---

18. Green, *New Testament Spirituality*, 209.

the disorderliness of the faith community. Eugene Peterson highlights the importance of staying the course:

> The churches of the Revelation show us that churches are not Victorian parlours where everything is always picked up and ready for guests. They are messy family rooms . . . They are not show rooms. They are living rooms, and if the persons living in them are sinners, there are going to be clothes scattered about, handprints on the woodwork, and mud on the carpet . . . St. John sees them simply as lampstands: they are places, locations, where the light of Christ is shown. They are not themselves the light.[19]

The salient point is that the church is inherently a fragile community due to the brokenness of its members; thus patience, long-suffering, and a humble spirit are always necessary to overcome the seeds of division which constantly lie beneath the surface.

There is also the call for churches to work together and not be caught up in a parochial spirit of competition and comparison. Whenever we cooperate in a spirit of unity we demonstrate to the larger public an attractive harmony of practice. Our own church community partners with a sister Baptist church to support the needs of the church in Bolivia through the remediation of Chagas disease, provision of preschool day care, assistance for children's education, and theological training for students and pastors. We also have received support for our community center from local churches of different denominations, which communicates unity and peace to our constituencies and the surrounding neighborhoods. When we commit to peacemaking we do not allow peripheral issues to derail the central mandate of expressing the love of Christ and working together for God's kingdom. In this regard there is a need for conversations to take place beyond church walls which bring together the larger body of Christ and express *shālôm* to a world caught up in division and enmity.

Interfaith Peacemaking

Connected to peace in the church is the importance of seeking peaceful relations with peoples of other faith traditions. In a world where there are only a handful of great faith traditions—Christianity, Judaism, Buddhism, Hinduism, and Islam—there is a great need for dialogue between the faith

---

19. Peterson, *Reversed Thunder*, 54.

traditions. The confrontational approach of attempting to convert one faith group to another does not instill peace but only antagonism. What is more fruitful is engagement along the lines of conversation, mutual understanding, and the pursuit of friendship. As an example, adjacent to our community center in Weston is an Ethiopian mosque representing 250 families. Over the years we have had conversations and worked together on issues concerning youth, violence, gangs, guns, and drugs; we know the Islamic community shares our concerns and seeks to address these problem areas. As we work together in addressing these needs a greater measure of peace is established in the neighborhood. Another example from my own context was sitting on the Jewish-Christian Dialogue Council for the city of Toronto. In this effort a number of rabbis and Christian ecumenical leaders met monthly to address issues of mutual concern. Throughout our times, we valued an irenic spirit of respect and mutual listening. Periodically, we agreed to address certain needs as seen by the council. However, the greatest accomplishment was simply meeting and building relationships of trust which diminished walls of misunderstanding and isolation.

It is this practical commitment to peacemaking that each Christian is invited to pursue in the journey of life. Friendships with individuals of different traditions can be nurtured at work, with neighbors, at school events, or in service projects in the community. It is by reaching across faith divides, at a local level, that a greater measure of peace is established in our cities and towns. Pursuing peace does not mean conformity on every issue; yet, it does flow best as we demonstrate the respectful attitudes of gentleness, kindness, patience, and self-control. Such an irenic spirit was demonstrated in President Obama's final address to the American people, when he encouraged individuals and communities to reach out to "the other" in a spirit of reflection and action. In reflection, he cited the great character in American literature Atticus Finch: "You never really understand a person until you consider things from his point of view . . . until you climb into his skin and walk around in it." In action, he advocated greater participation:

> So, you see, that's what our democracy demands. It needs you. Not just when there's an election, not just when your own narrow interest is at stake, but over the full span of a lifetime. If you're tired of arguing with strangers on the Internet, try talking with one of them in real life.[20]

---

20. Obama, Farewell Address.

It is through this combination of reflection and action that peacemaking moves beyond mere platitudes and becomes a life-changing force.

Earth Keeping and Justice Making

Peacemaking also includes our care and responsibility for the planet. The Scriptures are replete with assertions that the Earth is good, a gift from God, and that as his stewards we must care for it (Gen 1:26–27; 2:15). The psalmists sing of its beauty and abundance:

> You make springs gush forth in the valleys; they flow between the hills, giving drink to every wild animal; the wild asses quench their thirst. By the streams the birds of the air have their habitation; they sing among the branches. From your lofty abode you water the mountains; the earth is satisfied with the fruit of your work." (Ps 104:10–13)

> Sing to the Lord with thanksgiving . . . He covers the heavens with clouds, prepares rain for the earth, makes grass grow on the hills. He gives to the animals their food, and to the young ravens when they cry." (Ps 147:7–9)

Job adds his voice, declaring that even where no humans are found, the Earth sings of God's glory: "Who has cut a channel for the torrents of rain, and a way for the thunderbolt, to bring rain on a land where no one lives, on the desert, which is empty of human life, to satisfy the waste and desolate land, and to make the ground put forth grass" (Job 38:25–27).[21] God's *shālôm* is taken to an astounding level in the writings of Paul as he declares that the Earth will one day be completely renovated through the resurrection of Christ:

> For the creation waits with eager longing for the revealing of the children of God . . . that the creation itself will be set free from its bondage to decay and will obtain the freedom of the glory of the children of God. We know that the whole creation has been groaning in labour pains until now; and not only the creation, but we ourselves, who have the first fruits of the Spirit, groan inwardly while we wait for adoption, the redemption of our bodies. (Rom 8:19, 21–23)

---

21. See also Job 38–39; Ps 8:3–8; Gen 9:8–14; Eph 1:7–10.

These are just a few scriptures that address our need for tending the Earth that God has placed under our care.

We are not to abuse the Earth by rapaciously exploiting its resources and diminishing the planet's ecosystems. Unfortunately, such denigration is on the rise across a range of the Earth's systems, including land conversion and habitat destruction, species extinctions, land degradation, resource conversion, wastes and hazards production, global toxification, global warming, and human and cultural degradation.[22] Instead, we have a mandate to care for the Earth—its biodiversity, the oceans, the rivers, and the atmosphere—and not treat it as the "other" to simply be manipulated for economic gain. As Lewis Mumford notes, the community of faith is to actively work for the planet's healing by adopting a servant attitude towards the Earth:

> This benign transformation can happen on only one condition, and that is a hard one: namely that the life-negating ideals and methods of the power system be renounced, and that a conscious effort be made, at every level and in every kind of community, to live not for the sake of exalting power but for reclaiming this planet for life through mutual aid, loving association and biotechnic cultivation.[23]

The people of God need to be active participants in the healing of the Earth. It is self-defeating to argue that caring for the Earth is not the church's purview and that the church should remain focused on spiritual concerns. Bringing *shālôm* where there is an absence of *shālôm* is spiritual work, and this includes working for the *shālôm* of the planet.

Practically, how can we address this daunting task? The path forward is by taking small but intentional steps that lead us in the direction for the planet's healing. Constructive steps for a faith community might include instituting a recycling program if one does not already exist, picking up garbage in the church neighborhood, switching to cleaner fuels, initiating community gardens, or installing solar panels to produce green energy. These efforts demonstrate a caring attitude for the Earth and the immediate neighborhood the church serves. Faith communities can demonstrate a broader care for the Earth by supporting organizations such as A Rocha, the Evangelical Environmental Network, or the National Religious Partnership for the Environment, which promote, educate, and work for the care of the Earth. Individually, we can become active citizens in the pursuit of green initiatives by choosing

---

22. See DeWitt, *Environment and the Christian*, 14–23.
23. McDonagh, *Greening of the Church*, 164.

one area of engagement in which we have a significant concern. Through my passion for scuba diving I have developed a keen interest in the condition and protection of the world's water systems. Through different dive organizations I support environmental care for the world's coral reef systems and protection for the marine reserves of the Great Lakes. These funds support the critical ongoing work of marine education, protection of reef systems from degradation and overfishing, pollution controls for oceans and waterways, and an expansion of ocean reserves. Each of us have our own passions, so let us use that creative energy for the well-being of creation, and as we do so, extend the peace of God into his created order.[24]

Congruent with our concern for the planet is a desire for justice and compassion for the suffering. As Christians we cannot turn our backs on the plight of the marginalized and hurting while we live in plenty and ease. The prophets of Israel called the nation to stand alongside the poor in solidarity and they equally exhort the present generation to exhibit an awareness and an engagement for the amelioration of societal needs. We are called to advocate for the hurting and marginalized of the world. The prophets exhort us to speak and work on their behalf. Amos exclaims, "Let justice roll down like waters, and righteousness like an ever-flowing stream" (Amos 5:24); Micah declares, "He has told you, O mortal, what is good; and what does the Lord require of you but to do justice, and to love kindness, and to walk humbly with your God?" (Mic 6:8).[25]

Since our actions are shaped by the values we hold, we must consider the drivers that impact our decision making. Do our values mimic the avarice, competition, and "me first" attitudes propagated throughout the West? If this is the case, it is unlikely there is any available energy for peacemaking concerns on behalf of marginalized peoples. Indeed, we observe an absence of compassion driven by xenophobic fears revealed through isolationist policies and the commensurate rejection of refugees and immigrants. We see the turning away of the stranger rather than a welcoming and receptive spirit as taught by Christ. To this point K. C. Abraham raises two salient questions for the reshaping of our values: "To whom are we listening?" and "Whose interests do we represent?"[26] As we contemplate these questions he encourages us to engage the "enabling power" modeled

---

24. See Isa 11:1–11.
25. See also Hos 4:2–3; Amos 2:6–8; Mic 6:11–12.
26. Abraham, "Theological Response to the Ecological Crisis," 75.

by Jesus and reject "the power that dominates, manipulates and exploits."[27] Through the implementation of such a process new values can be formed that foster compassionate action and raise up the communities that have been ignored, trodden down, and manipulated for personal gain.

We enter into this work because Jesus is our peace and he calls us to pursue the kingdom mandate of making peace in a broken world. Such a work is daunting but it begins by "turning our own hearts around" and embracing a lifestyle that follows the ways of the compassionate Christ.[28] Jesus is the great Sender, and we are his sent ones, who are empowered with the same Spirit that filled our Lord: "The Spirit of the Lord is upon me, because he has anointed me to bring good news to the poor. He has sent me to proclaim release to the captives and recovery of sight to the blind, to let the oppressed go free, to proclaim the year of the Lord's favour" (Luke 4:18–19). As we collectively take up the cause of peace, we radiate Christ's love as his passionate bride and become a manifestation of the *shālôm* of God.

Questions for Reflection

1. Paul uses the three metaphors of citizens, family, and temple as ways of explaining our deep connection with Abba. Which of these metaphors resonates with you the most? Why do you think this is the case?

2. What are the roadblocks you face in pursuing peace within the faith community? Are there steps you can take that might help in addressing these challenges?

3. What area aligns with your interests in the work of peacemaking for the planet? How can you engage this area of concern in practical ways?

4. Standing in solidarity with those who are marginalized is a biblical injunction reiterated in the Minor Prophets (Micah 6:8; Amos 5:21–24). In what ways can you personally and your church family collectively identify with the hurting in your community and take steps to improve their lot?

---

27. Abraham, "Theological Response to the Ecological Crisis," 76.
28. Rossum, *Reinhabiting the Earth*, 68–69.

5

The Spirituality of Mystery

Ephesians 3:1–13

"The goal of faith is not to create a set of immutable, rationalized, precisely defined and defendable beliefs to preserve forever. It is to recover a relationship with God. He offers us a person and a relationship; we want rules and a format. He offers us security through risk; we want safety through certainty. He offers us unity and community; we want unanimity and institutions. And it does no good to point fingers because none of us desires too much light. All of us want God to behave Himself in our lives, to touch this area but leave that one alone, to empower us here but let us run things ourselves over there."

Daniel Taylor, The Myth of Certainty

"This is the reason that I Paul am a prisoner for Christ Jesus—
    for surely you have already heard of the commission of God's grace that was given to me
        for you,
and how **the mystery was made known to me by revelation,**
        as I wrote above in a few words,
        a reading of which will enable you to perceive my understanding
            of **the mystery**
            of **Christ.**

In former generations this mystery was not made known to humankind,
> as it has now been revealed to his holy apostles and prophets by
> the Spirit:
> that is, the Gentiles have become fellow-heirs,
>> members of the same body,
>> and sharers in the promise in Christ Jesus through the gospel.

Of this gospel I have become a servant according to the gift of God's grace
> that was given to me by the working of his power.
> Although I am the very least of all the saints,
>> this grace was given to me to bring to the Gentiles the news of
>> the boundless
>> riches of Christ,

and to **make everyone see what is the plan of the mystery hidden for ages**
> in God who created all things:
> so that through the church the wisdom of God
>> in its rich variety might now be made known to the rulers
>> and authorities in the
>> heavenly places.

This was in accordance with the eternal purpose
> that he has carried out in Christ Jesus our Lord,
> in whom we have access to God in boldness and confidence through
> faith in him.

I pray therefore that you may not lose heart over my sufferings for you;
> they are your glory."   (Ephesians 3:1–13)

Years ago, I set out on a road trip from Toronto to Key West. As I passed through the immigration services at Buffalo the officer asked the usual, "Where are you going?" My response of "Key West" piqued his interest. "Key West! I haven't heard that one in a long time! What are you going to do down there?"

I enthusiastically responded, "I'm going to dive up and down the Florida Keys!"

There was a pregnant pause, as the officer studied me and my dive gear, tanks and all, in the back of the CRV. Finally, he leaned forward and deliberately said, "Well, you be careful down there, with all those sharks," and handed back my passport.

After several weeks of driving, camping, and delightful diving, including the Outer Banks of North Carolina and the World War II wrecks adjacent to Kitty Hawk and Cape Hatteras, I arrived at my final destination, the laid-back town of Key West, famous for its conch house neoclassical architecture, and the house of Earnest Hemingway, replete with the descendants of his polydactyl cats! I visited the museum of Mel Fisher, with its holdings of golden artifacts, which he found on the Spanish galleons of the Santa Margarita and Nuestra Señora de Atocha, sunk during a violent hurricane in 1622.

Fisher's story is incredulous—one of determination, grit, and patience! Fisher and his team hunted for the lost galleons every day for sixteen long years, repeating the mantra, "Today is the day!" Finally, on a summer day in 1985 he discovered the treasure, including 100,000 "pieces of eight" (a haulage of forty tons of gold and silver) with a value of 450 million dollars! Finding the treasure of jewels, gold, and silver was most impressive. But what struck me the most was his perseverance in solving the mystery of the two lost galleons. The sinking of the treasure ships was known for centuries, and even that they lay in the vicinity of Key West. The exact location, however, remained a mystery, covered with four centuries of shifting sands! Fisher knew the treasure lay on the sea bottom somewhere between Key West and Cuba, and his goal was to keep searching until it was found. Like Noah of old, Fisher faced his share of taunting from naysayers, as day by day he sailed his disfigured boat out to sea, reconfigured with an oversized vacuum cleaner, its hoses on deck, enabling the divers to shift the sea floor sands. Fisher was unabated. He believed in the mystery of the catch and continued his search until finally discovering the treasure trove on July 20, 1985.

As we continue reading Paul's Letter to the Ephesians, we learn that he also believed in a great mystery, and that the clue for its understanding was found in the death and resurrection of Jesus Christ. It is to this mystery and the apostle's role in revealing it that we turn now.

A Mysterious Encounter

Paul writes his letter from a Roman jail cell and acknowledges that he is there principally because of his ministry to the Gentiles (Eph 3:1).[1] Reminding his readers of the divine call which he experienced on the road to Damascus, Paul writes, "Surely you have already heard of the commission of God's grace that was given to me for you" (3:2). His use of the word *oikonomia*, or "commission" or "plan," speaks to his life-changing encounter with the risen Christ on the road to Damascus. Luke records this story three times in his writing of Acts due to its critical nature. The first account is as follows:

> Now as he was going along and approaching Damascus, suddenly a light from heaven flashed around him. He fell to the ground and heard a voice saying to him, 'Saul, Saul, why do you persecute me?' He asked, 'Who are you, Lord?' The reply came, 'I am Jesus, whom you are persecuting. But get up and enter the city, and you will be told what you are to do.'" (Acts 9: 3–6)[2]

The Damascus road experience was a shocking intervention which reversed his path and changed his life forever. Paul turned his life around from being an enemy of Jesus, zealously persecuting the early church, to the embodiment of a dedicated apostle of the long-awaited Messiah. As Paul comes to a deeper understanding of his stunning encounter with Christ, he draws out the nuances of what the "mystery" means in terms of Christ's work for both the church and humankind as a whole. It is worth noting that the word *mystērion*, or "mystery," occurs six times in Ephesians, including four times in the immediate context (3:2, 4, 5, 9). Obviously, the apostle is overwhelmed by the profound nature of the Christ-event. Paul experiences the mystery of Christ's presence as a remarkable act of grace demonstrating his passionate love, forgiveness, and mercy, for which the apostle to the Gentiles is forever grateful.

A closer reading of Luke's accounts of Paul's conversion story reveals that Christ has been impressing the apostle with the truth over a season of time, as evidenced in Paul's own defense before King Agrippa. He recalls Christ's words, "Saul, Saul, why are you persecuting me? It hurts you to kick against the goads" (Acts 26:14). The word "persecuting" can also be translated

---

1. Many commentators argue that Paul was a prisoner in Rome during the reign of Nero. See Stott, *God's New Society*, 114–15; Wood, "Ephesians," 44.

2. See also Acts 22:6–11; 26:12–17.

"resisting" and is colorfully illustrated in the scene by the sheep or goat kicking back against the shepherd's "goad."[3] Christ has been speaking to Saul and he has been resisting his voice, but thankfully "the hound of heaven" pursues its prey undauntedly and eventually corrals its desired soul.[4]

It strikes me that Paul is not alone in resisting the Divine Spirit, as part of us wants to hear from God and another part does not. As Henri Nouwen reminds us, "God wants all our attention and we are not sure we want to give it."[5] If this is the case, it behooves us to consider the possibility that we are kicking against God's overtures and identify the reasons for doing so. The good news is that the King of Heaven does not give up but continually draws and woos us to himself in love. On a separate occasion Paul makes just this point as he pens encouraging words to his young charge Timothy: "If we are faithless, he remains faithful—for he cannot deny himself" (2 Tim 2:13). It is this promise which continues to sustain us even in times of resistance and spiritual fragility.

Unveiling the Mystery of Christ

Paul raises the theme of a divine mystery in his other writings, most notably in his First Letter to the Corinthians: "When I came to you, brothers and sisters, I did not come proclaiming the mystery of God to you in lofty words or wisdom. For I decided to know nothing among you except Jesus Christ, and him crucified" (1 Cor 2:1–2). In this passage the mystery refers to the salvific impact of Christ's crucifixion, which the Jewish community found to be a blasphemous concept and the Romans considered simply as foolishness.

In our present letter the apostle understands the mystery to refer to God's will that was hidden in time past but has now been revealed through the death and resurrection of Jesus Christ (Eph 3:5). Commentators Talbot and Stott remind readers that the specific edge of the mystery relates to the formation of a new people, comprised of Jew and Gentile together, woven into a new society of God.[6] Paul refers to Gentile believers being fully received into the community of faith as "fellow heirs, members of

---

3. See Davey, *Climbing the Spiritual Mountain*, 12, The Amplified Bible qualifies "persecuting" as meaning "to offer vain and perilous resistance."
4. Thompson, "Hound of Heaven," title.
5. Roderick, *Beloved*, 42.
6. Talbot, *Ephesians and Colossians*, 98; Stott, *God's New Society*, 117.

the same body, and sharers in the promise in Christ" (3:6) Each of these designations—"co-heirs," "concorporate," co-sharers"—Stott observes, share the prefix *syn*, or "with," reminding the Gentiles of their connection with Jewish believers.[7] This truth is groundbreaking as it proclaims that Jews and Gentiles form one new people transcending the myriad of differences of diverse cultures, religions, and ethnicities. Abba is weaving together a brilliant tapestry of individuals from all nations and is forming one new humanity through the person and work of Jesus Christ. In past epochs the nation of Israel represented God's chosen people, but now the *laos*, or "people," of God is no longer constrained by ethnicity or geography through the reconciling work of Jesus Christ.

Paul stipulates that his apostolic vocation is "to bring the Gentiles the news of the boundless riches of Christ" (3:8) and that this proclamation reveals the "mystery hidden for ages in God who created all things" (3:9). The denouement consists in the revelation being expressed through "the church" and that even the heavenly powers are astounded at the birth of Abba's new race (3:10). The *ecclesia*, the church, is revealed through the tension of unity (3:6) and diversity (3:10) as many peoples comprise one body but express their gifts in rich and diverse ways. The apostle enthuses that "the wisdom of God in its rich variety might now be made known" (3:10). Later in the letter he adds, "But each . . . was given grace according to the measure of Christ's gift" (4:7). The result of this gathering is the creation of a new people manifested through a rich kaleidoscope of colors, expressions, and spiritual gifts. Stott provides an eloquent description of this new creation as he writes, "The church as a multi-racial, multi-cultural community is like a beautiful tapestry. Its members come from a wide range of colourful backgrounds. No other human community resembles it. Its diversity and harmony are unique. It is God's new society."[8]

This church is empowered by God and is graciously granted the role of partnering with him for his kingdom on planet Earth (Eph 1:19–23). Furthermore, Paul also argues that the church reveals God's mysterious workings to the "authorities in the heavenly places" (3:10). The new people of God are given the essential task of representing Christ to the masses. It is an exalted vocation which funds every Christian with meaning and purpose regardless of the station one holds within the human story. Before anything else, we are followers of Jesus and his ambassadors to the world,

---

7. See Stott, *God's New* Society, 117.
8. Stott, *God's New Society*, 123.

which instills a fundamental dignity for everyone who bears his name. The divine mandate beckons us to become mature, integrated individuals who bear spiritual fruit as we align ourselves with his purposes in everyday living. Keating refers to this kind of spiritual maturity as "mental egoic consciousness" in which one embraces a lived relationship with Abba revealed in true love for one's neighbor and the oppressed of the Earth.[9]

In light of this blessed journey, it is most unfortunate if we dismiss our role as active participants in the church of Christ to pursue secondary matters or because we find communal life too vexing. Bonhoeffer describes such spiritual complacency as he writes:

> If we do not give thanks daily for the Christian fellowship in which we have been placed, even when there is no great experience, no discoverable riches, but much weakness, small faith, and difficulty; if on the contrary, we only keep complaining to God that everything is so paltry and petty, so far from what we expected, then we hinder God from letting our fellowship grow according to the measure and riches which are there for us all in Jesus Christ.[10]

The truth remains that we are called to a life together and spiritual formation takes place within the dynamics of communal life. In spite of the church's observable weaknesses our spiritual journey cannot be limited to our individual faith narrative (Acts 2:42).[11]

Paul concludes this section by affirming the exhilarating truth that through Christ "we have access to the Father in boldness and confidence" (Eph 3:12). In the Greco-Roman world the gods were understood to be capricious and self-serving; therefore, access to them was never sure.[12] To counter this common understanding Paul affirms the truth that in Christ we can approach God on a daily basis and know that we will be received as his beloved children. The writer of Hebrews reinforces this point as he declares that Christ is our great high priest "who has passed through the heavens" and "in every respect has been tested as we are, yet without sin," and for these reasons he is able to lead us into the presence of Abba with confidence and boldness (Heb 4:14–16). As a result, we do not have to earn God's approval as though it is through our own effort that we stand before him. Our own efforts are doomed to failure in our fragility

---

9. Keating, *Foundations for Centering Prayer*, 165.
10. Bonhoeffer, *Life Together*, 29.
11. See also Green and Stevens, *New Testament Spirituality*, 76–90.
12. Wright, *Paul for Everyone*, 37.

and with our ego-driven mindset and selfish desires. Knowing the human condition, Christ charted the course to victory, and by faith in his person we follow his lead. As Melancthon understood, "To know Christ, is to know his benefits."[13]

The unit ends with the apostle praying that the community of faith will "not lose heart" over his imprisonment or because of his sufferings (Eph 3:13). He encourages his audience to keep going to Abba, knowing that the Father holds them all in his loving arms. Such a word continues to be relevant as often we do lose heart. Life is strenuous! We face hurdles at every juncture through sickness, financial pressure, loss of employment, anxiety for loved ones, as well as a myriad of other concerns. Left to our own resources, we do, indeed, become discouraged. Thankfully, the Scriptures draw us back to the gracious hand of the Father, who is "the giver of every good gift" (Jas 1:17) and who "satisfies our every need according to his riches in Christ Jesus (Phil 4:19).

The Illogical Call of the Mystery[14]

The apex of God's mysterious work in the world is found in Jesus Christ, who establishes a new humanity committed to the imitation of God through a lifestyle of sacrificial love and service (Eph 5:1–2).[15] The locus of the mystery is found in the life, death, and resurrection of Jesus, who as the risen Lord sends the Holy Spirit to indwell and empower the church for the ongoing work of God. Understanding on a macro level the clear strokes of the salvation story, there remains at a micro level an elusive dimension for fully understanding humankind's participation in the divine-human relationship.

Jesus makes this point in his conversation with Nicodemus as he argues that "no one can see the kingdom of God without being born from above" (John 3:3). The Pharisee is caught off guard by this declaration and ponders aloud how this new birth might be: "Can one enter a second time into the mother's womb and be born again?" (3:4). Jesus references the nature of the wind in that one cannot precisely know its source; "so it is with everyone who is born of the Spirit" (3:8). The implied conclusion of the dialogue is that we understand much about spiritual matters but still a great deal remains

---

13. Martin, *Ephesians, Colossians*, 114.
14. "Illogical call" is a phrase by Nouwen in Roderick, *Beloved*, 37.
15. See also Col 1:26–27; 4:3.

unknown. A disservice is committed to the story of faith if we reduce it to a step-by-step formula as we would a math equation. As Henri Nouwen observes, there is a great need for faith when it comes to receiving the mystery of the gospel, which cannot be defined with absolute precision:

> That's why I say it's an enormous act of faith to believe that if you start listening, you will hear something; or that if you enter into solitude, you will find intimacy; or that when you are silent you are not going to be dead silent, it'll be a lively silence. It is an act of faith that there is a God who loves us. I can't prove that to you, I can't even argue with that.

In this mystery, Nouwen goes on to suggest, there are signposts that point to what we can suspect.

> I can only say that those who have entered with me into solitude, prayer, communion, and contemplative community start loving each other, start forgiving each other, and start living. They discover that the grace to do that is a grace that transcends us; that there is someone else who sent us Jesus. They sense that God is not going to leave us.[16]

The dilemma we face is when we understand certainty to be a corollary for our understanding of spiritual concerns. It is frequently expressed in terms of banishing doubt to the trashcan and decrying its value in the journey of faith. As Daniel Taylor recognizes "Much of the church has [also] sold out to the myth of certainty . . . [the] ultimate goal is the same: an unquestionable, undoubtable foundation on which to base all subsequent claims."[17] While it is true that we desire a sure foundation for ultimate concerns, it is not to be gained by eradicating the essential role that mystery and uncertainty play. The psalmists demonstrate a willingness to speak of doubt and the questioning of God's ways. "How long, O Lord? Will you forget me forever? How long will you hide your face from me? How long must I bear pain in my soul, and have sorrow in my heart all day long? How long shall my enemy be exalted over me?" (Ps 13:1–2), laments one psalm writer. Another complains, "Such are the wicked; always at ease, they increase in riches. All in vain I have kept my heart clean and washed my hands in innocence. For all day long I have been plagued, and am punished every morning" (Ps 73:12–14). Job muses about God's mysterious ways with humankind:

---

16. Roderick, *Beloved*, 41–42.
17. Taylor, *Myth of Certainty*, 78–79.

> Why is life given to a man whose way is hidden, whom God has hedged in? For sighing has become my daily food; my groans pour out like water. What I feared has come upon me; what I dreaded has happened to me. I have no peace, no quietness; I have no rest, but only turmoil. (Job 3:23–26)

We know that over time Job works his way through to a place of trusting God, but that point does not erase the challenges of the journey (Job 42:5–6).

There is an element of "unknowing" when it comes to our relationship with "the Holy."[18] We do not completely understand the ways of Abba and should not pretend that we do or insist on an absolute degree of certainty on every issue—even as Jesus admits to not knowing everything! (Mark 13:32). We do not live presciently; thus, we need to accept mystery and a degree of uncertainty as we push ahead in our life journey. Further, by definition, faith requires an element of doubt—or at least mystery—or it would not be needed at all. As the writer of Hebrews observes, "Now faith is the assurance of things hoped for, the conviction of things not seen" (Heb 11:1).

Acknowledgement of mystery is not a sign of weakness or an indicator of a person's inadequate theology. Rather, it is an honest recognition of the human condition, as revealed in the desperate father's prayer for his ailing son, "Lord I believe, help my unbelief!" (Mark 9:24). In fact, if one incorporates doubt into faith rather than rejecting it outright, its inherent tension might actually serve one's faith.[19] As we draw our questions back into our walk of faith instead of dismissing them, we reinforce the qualities of endurance and perseverance which are needed for "taking up our cross and following Jesus" (Matt 16:24); that is, we feel its weight—a heavy, rough beam of wood—cutting into our shoulders and back. It is a burden—not an entertaining stroll in the park. As Taylor summarizes his argument, "Doubt makes its claims, even daily, and they are respected, but they do not determine the character of my life."[20] We are able to intertwine the reality of mystery and doubt into our relationship with Abba and do so confidently, knowing that he guides and sustains us as we make our way through the challenges of life.

In Paul's parallel Letter to the Colossians he writes that our lives are both "hidden with Christ in God" (Col 4:3) and that Christ is our very "life"!

---

18. Walsh, ed., *Cloud of Unknowing*, title.
19. Taylor, *Myth of Certainty*, 80.
20. Taylor, *Myth of Certainty*, 81.

(4:4). He is not only King, Shepherd, Comforter, Counselor, Warrior—he is our very life! As a result, we are invited to get on with living our new life, which encapsulates mystery, mission, vocation, community, and purpose. There is an adventure to be embraced which begins now and continues to unfold through the coming ages. We are encouraged to confidently live out the mystery of Christ and to know that he is there for us at every turn we face in the road of life. We do not need to know the precise pattern for every step we take; rather, we press on, knowing that Christ travels with us and enables us to face every trial in a spirit of equanimity.

Living the Mystery

We are called as the passionate bride of Christ to enter into the mystery of Abba by receiving his overtures of love and responding in kind by wholeheartedly loving him. A fitting place to enter this mysterious union is the community of the church. We take our cues from Paul, who views the church to be Christ's bride (Eph 5:31–32), deeply loved by him and essential for his work in the world. Rather than ignoring or deriding the church's value, we are invited to embrace it and use our gifts as members of his body (4:7–8).[21] Since God works through his collective people, it is incumbent on every believer to fully participate if the church is to work effectively. When believers drop out due to discouragement, boredom, or internal conflict, the church is weakened and kingdom work is diminished. By isolating ourselves we also miss out on a community of people that help us to understand the mysterious workings of God through the intertwining of our lives. Instead, we are encouraged to get involved and to use our spiritual gifts for the building up of Christ's body. As we come to know and hear the stories of other believers we will be both amazed at the incredible diversity of God's people and inspired by their cogent testimonies.

A second field for entering God's mystery is to become aware of his presence within the created order. The apostle Paul reminds us of this truth as he writes, "For since the creation of the world God's invisible qualities—his eternal power and divine nature—have been clearly seen, being understood from what has been made" (Rom 1:20). Too often our gaze is turned inward and we miss the beauty that his creation reveals. We are invited to open our eyes to truly see the wonder of creation. In his autobiography *Surprised by Joy*, C. S. Lewis speaks of his daily walks in the English countryside,

---

21. See Wright, *Paul*, 78.

which became opportunities to explore life's meaning, periodically acting as "signposts" that led him into divine truth.[22]

Similarly, creation, "charged with the grandeur of God," acts as a conduit to enable us to experience the presence of God.[23] I was impressed with just this fact on a recent family trip to Ucluelet, where we spent time scanning the night sky from a cottage perched high over the Pacific Ocean. Our viewings were aided by the use of a bedraggled telescope serving as a living room prop in our rented quarters. After a rejigging of the forgotten instrument, we focused our attention on the planet Saturn and were rewarded with a glorious sight to behold—a stunning white globe circled by its rings of ice and rocky particles! As I peered through the telescope (mimicking the first viewing of Galileo in 1610!) I felt like I could reach out and touch the little white ball with my fingertips. It was a spiritual moment as I connected with our distant sister planet 1.2 billion kilometers away! The invitation to explore God's creation remains as he beckons us through his quiet whispers to enjoy the wonders of his divine presence.

Furthermore, as we intentionally engage God's creation—walking, hiking, camping, birding, driving (maybe diving!)—we can anticipate holy moments, revealing to our hearts and minds the mysteries of God. St. Francis's "Canticle of the Creatures" inspires us as we move in this direction:

> Most high, all powerful, good Lord,
> All praise be yours, all glory, all honour and all blessing . . .
>
> All praise be yours, my Lord, in all your creatures,
> Especially Sir Brother Sun who brings the day;
> And light you give us through him . . .
>
> All praise be yours, my Lord, for Sister Moon and the Stars;
> In the heavens you have made them, bright and precious and fair.
>
> All praise be yours, my Lord, for Brother Wind and the Air,
> And fair and stormy and every kind of weather
> By which you nourish everything you have made.
>
> All praise be yours, my Lord, for Sister Water;
> She is so useful and lowly, so precious and pure.

---

22. Lewis, *Surprised by Joy*, 155–56.
23. See Gerard Manley Hopkins, "God's Grandeur."

All praise be yours, my Lord, for Brother Fire
By whom you brighten the night.
How beautiful he is, how gay, robust and strong!

All praise be yours, my Lord, for Sister Earth, our mother
Who feeds us, rules us and produces all sorts of fruits
And coloured flowers and herbs . . .[24]

    A third opportunity for perceiving the divine mystery is through the arts, which hold potential for leading us deeper into what has been named the *mysterium tremendum*—awe-inspiring mystery. In his works on effective worship in the contemporary church, Robert Webber reminds us of familiar studies in neuropsychology that highlight the importance of the right side of the brain and its capacity for responding to "symbolic forms of communication."[25] He contrasts "enlightenment communication," with its emphasis on reading, writing, clarity, explanation, and linear sequence, with "post-enlightenment communication," which highlights image, experience, music, environment, intuition, and emotional knowledge.[26] He notes that Protestantism has traditionally concentrated on the brain's left-sided capacities, which include logic, reason, and propositional learning, with less emphasis upon the intuitive and evocative dimensions, which flow from the right side of the brain.[27]

    When we embrace creative impulses that strengthen right-brain capacities, we receive immediate dividends for hearing and appreciating new dimensions of spiritual truth. The arts—music, drama, dance, the visual arts—in all their multiple forms can become a forceful channel for God's activity in our lives. Carolyn Arends suggests how this might work: "[The] arts help us train to pay attention . . . receptivity to art teaches us to focus, to press beyond surface impressions, and to look, listen, smell, touch and taste with care, thought and patience." Beyond paying attention, she posits that "the arts help us train in longing . . . [that] the arts can be an important ally in recovering some of God's vision for the world."[28] C. S. Lewis, author of the famous Narnia Chronicles, in his essay "On Three Ways of Writing

---

24. Rossum, *Reinhabiting the Earth*, 145–46.
25. Webber, *Worship Is a Verb*, 21.
26. Webber, *Worship Is a Verb*, 27.
27. Webber, *Worship Is a Verb*, 26.
28. Arends, "Artful Discipleship," 30.

for Children," commends the art form of the fairy tale for the longing it creates in a child:

> [F]airy land arouses a longing for he knows not what. It stirs and troubles him (to his life-long enrichment) with the dim sense of something beyond his reach and, far from dulling or emptying the actual world, gives it a new dimension of depth. He does not despise real woods because he has read of enchanted woods: the reading makes all real woods a little enchanted. This is a special kind of longing.[29]

Lewis goes on to identify this longing as "an *askesis*, a spiritual exercise."[30] As both these authors have suggested, nurturing "right-sided" brain activity increases our capacity for understanding and receiving spiritual truth.

Creative insights may come through a piece of music, a sculpture, a photograph, a painting, a dance, a theatrical scene. Any of these artistic expressions (and more) have the capacity to reveal transformative spiritual truth. I recall an experience when I traveled with my brother through central Turkey, retracing the steps of the apostle Paul. We had heard that Whirling Dervishes were performing nearby so we found our way to a twelfth-century caravansary to take in their meditative dance. As we observed the interplay of their graceful movement, we were drawn into their whirling meditation as they offered their praise to God. It became for us a serendipitous signpost declaring the mystery of Abba and his desire to connect with our own spiritual aspirations. As James writes, "Or do you suppose that it is for nothing that the scripture says, 'God yearns jealously for the spirit that he has made to dwell in us'" (Jas 4:5).

As we intentionally open our eyes, we enter a sacred space where the tension of paradox, mystery, and faith coalesces into a dynamic relationship with the living God. It may happen through the arts, the splendor of creation, dynamic stories from the faith community, or a myriad of other ways of hearing his still, small voice. Finally, rather than being dismayed that the journey of faith is as variated and nuanced as the universe God created, it is up to us to choose to embrace the *mysterium tremendum* as a window for experiencing God's abundance. Through it all we are supported by the complementary pathways of the faith community to explore and enter into the mysteries of God as the beloved bride of his only begotten Son.

---

29. Lewis, "On Three Ways of Writing for Children," 29–30.
30. Lewis, "On Three Ways of Writing for Children," 30.

Questions for Reflection

1. Paul maintains an elevated ecclesiology, viewing the church as the new humanity that incorporates people from every nation and is instrumental in the work of God's kingdom. Unfortunately, many Christians today do not share his enthusiasm. Why do you think this is the case? Are there steps we can take to foster a greater zeal for the local church? Is there a need to reconsider our own participation and commitment to the church of Christ?

2. Daniel Taylor argues that mystery remains an essential part of our relationship with Abba and this is reinforced by the utilization of the word *mystērion* in Ephesians. Paul describes our present experience of knowing Jesus as "seeing the glory of the Lord as though reflected in a mirror" (2 Cor 3:18); hence, for Paul, mystery is not viewed negatively, but positively, evoking possibilities that contribute to the believer's final hope. Is there a way we can embrace the reality of mystery in a way which energizes our relationship with Abba?

3. We have seen that both the arts and creation are vehicles for experiencing the wonder of God's love. C. S. Lewis called such moments "signposts" towards God. Reflect on your life journey and note any signposts that come to mind. In your journal write down ways that you have been impacted during those *kairos* moments.

6

Crazy Love

Ephesians 3:14–21

"When the evening of this life comes we shall be judged on Love."

St. John of the Cross

"The Mystics, to give them their short familiar name, are men and women who insist that they know for certain the presence and activity of that which they call the Love of God."

Evelyn Underhill, The Love of God

"For this reason I bow my knees before the Father,
  from whom every family in heaven and on earth takes its name.
I pray that, according to the riches of his glory,
  he may grant that you may be strengthened in your inner being with power through his Spirit,
  and that Christ may dwell in your hearts through faith,
    *as **you are being rooted and grounded in love.***

*I pray that **you may have the power to comprehend, with all the saints,***
  what is the breadth and length and height and depth,
    and to know the love of Christ that surpasses knowledge,
  so that you may be filled with all the fullness of God."

"Now to him who by the power at work within us is able to accomplish abundantly far more than all we can ask or imagine,

> *to him be glory in the church and in Christ Jesus to all generations, for ever and ever. Amen."*   *(Ephesians 3:14–21)*

The film *A United Kingdom* tells the story of Seretse Khama, heir to the throne of Bechuanaland, who is finishing up his university studies in England just after the Second World War. During his time of study he falls in love with a young woman, Ruth Williams, and they eventually marry in spite of her father's virulent racial disapproval. The tensions concerning their marriage are intensified when they return to his African homeland. His uncle, the acting regent, does not accept his Caucasian wife and demands that he divorce her and marry a Bamangwato princess. Seretse flatly refuses his uncle's demands, creating a schism in the family and unrest among the people over his marital union. Things become even more complicated as the British government sides with his uncle and banishes Seretse from his own country due to fears of upsetting the apartheid government of South Africa, where Britain has vested interests in the nation's gold trade. As the story unfolds, Seretse and Ruth are slowly able to win the people over in spite of his banishment, and the English Parliament allows him to return home to oversee the process of Bechuanaland becoming the democratic country of Botswana. Through it all Seretse and Ruth share a devoted and enlivening love which overcomes daunting barriers and serendipitously leads to the transformation of an entire nation.

The remarkable love of Sir Seretse Khama and Ruth Williams Khama casts our eyes in the direction of God's unfailing and immutable love for his church. Abba's love for us in this very moment is as profound as any future charity we will experience in the splendor of heaven. Abba's lovingkindness is unchanging, immense, and unfathomable, even as Evelyn Underhill observes, in the words of Abbé de Tourville,

> Remember, that God loves your soul, not in some aloof, impersonal way, but passionately, with the adoring cherishing love of a parent for a child. The out-pouring of His Holy Spirit is really the outpouring of His love, surrounding and penetrating your little soul with a peaceful, joyful delight in His creature: tolerant, peaceful love full of long-suffering and gentleness, working quietly,

able to wait for results, faithful, devoted, without variableness or shadow of turning. Such is the charity of God.[1]

It is true that our perception of God's never-ending love is muted by the human overcast which so often covers our souls. Life's challenges often derail us and we lose connection with Abba's exhilarating first love. It is not surprising then that Paul draws the first half of his letter to a close with a prayer which exults in God's love for his beloved children. He is helping us remember our status as Abba's beloved.

Belonging to God

Overjoyed by God's gracious work, the apostle falls to his knees, addressing God as his Abba and praying for his spiritual children. Paul kneels before God, whom he calls *Patēr*, or "Father," which is a Greek translation for the Aramaic *Abba* employed by Jesus—the same "Our Father" addressed in the Lord's Prayer (Matt 6:9). As noted earlier, Paul also uses the title Abba in his prayers and encourages us to do so as well in our conversation with God (Gal 4:6; Rom 8:15). Paul affirms that the Creator of the universe is also our loving Father or Abba, who can be approached in confidence even as a young child runs to her father in need. In his sheltering and faithful love as Abba, he is absolutely with us in every situation enabling us to proceed in a spirit of calm repose.

It is a natural movement for Paul to take up a reverent posture in preparation for this act of intercession. Through his example we are reminded to make the connection between body, mind, and spirit as we participate in the action of prayer. Conversing with Abba is not simply a mental spiritual construct; it is a dialogue that flows from an embodied response. This is especially apparent in times of spiritual dryness, when physical actions such as kneeling, raising outstretched hands, or prostrating ourselves before God reinforce our aspirations for spiritual intimacy.[2]

As Paul prays, he acknowledges that "every family in heaven and on earth" (Eph 3:15) finds its source in the creative power of the Father, highlighted by linking *patēr*, or "Father," and *patria*, or "every family," with "a deliberate play on words," as Stott points out.[3] The connection between our

---

1. Underhill, *Love of God*, 43–44.
2. See Webber, *Planning Blended Worship*, 47.
3. Stott, *God's New Society*, 133.

loving Father and every human family reminds us that God's love flows amidst every family unit whether we are consciously aware of this truth or not. This lively love is expressed through a natural familial tenderness that we readily observe as parents love their children with a passionate resoluteness regardless of religion or faith practice. As people of faith we are invited to reflect God's love in all of our relationships and to do it through an attitude of sacrificial love. Doing so, we become stepping-stones which point others to the love of God, and as Dorothy Day once mused, "make it easier for people to come to know God's love."[4]

We create unnecessary hurdles for ourselves when we look to other sources for our sense of well-being and purpose in life instead of turning towards God's love. We are quick to seek our sense of belonging in our race, group, nationality, or socioeconomic class, which locates our hope on the shifting sands of time and culture.[5] The mores of competition and comparison weigh heavily on us as we scrutinize our progress with that of our neighbors. Popularity, fame, financial success, beauty, intellectual prowess, and societal recognition all ring powerfully in our minds as we struggle to be the best at something and earn the accolades of our culture. Unfortunately, rarely are we preeminent at anything! Such aspirations condemn us to a life of disappointment, falling far short of our intrinsic longing for infinite love and acceptance. Furthermore, engaging in competition or comparison only distracts us from resting in Abba's deep-seated love.

In contrast, we have the option to respond to Paul's declaration that "we belong to God." We are his beloved children! We do not have to earn our acceptance by passing through all kinds of hoops and cultural rituals. We are loved by Abba and accepted by him though our participation in Jesus Christ and nothing more is needed. If we maintain our focus on God's love as it is manifested in the life, death, and resurrection of Jesus, we can enjoy a liberating serenity. In this regard, a daily practice of "re-membering" that we belong to God is most helpful and may be nurtured by beginning our days in quiet meditation, simply repeating the phrase, "I belong to God." As we replace our previous interior messages—"I am not good enough" and "I have to earn my acceptance"—with the new ones—"I am loved by God" and "I belong to God"—we gradually renew our minds and establish our acceptance of Abba's profound love. Gustavo Gutiérrez alludes to such a divine connection through the words of a martyred Bolivian priest, "'Train

---

4. Day, *Selected Writings*, 213.
5. See Keating, *Foundations for Centering Prayer*, 157–60.

us, Lord, to fling ourselves upon the impossible, for behind the impossible is your grace and your presence; we cannot fall into emptiness.'" Gutiérrez completes the priest's prayer with his own affirmation, "This is what Job did: he flung himself upon the impossible and into an enigmatic future. And in this effort he met the Lord."[6] Likewise, we can achieve the same miracle in our celebration of Abba's deep love for us.

Strengthened by God

As Paul intercedes for the Ephesians he specifically prays that they will "be strengthened in [their] inner beings with power through [God's] Spirit" (Eph 3:16). These words introduce a new dimension to his petition. Up to this point he has focused on what the community has received in Christ.[7] But at this juncture Paul calls for spiritual growth, an interior strengthening by the Spirit which enables one to become firmly established in the faith relationship. It is not sufficient to seek a relationship with Jesus and after a period of time to settle for the status quo. Rather, we are invited to go deeper and plumb the depths of our spiritual union with the triune God. The apostle describes this journey of spiritual growth with the metaphors of "being rooted" and "being grounded in love" (3:17). "Rooted" is an agricultural term, referring to plants sending their roots deep into the soil, nurturing growth and fruitfulness. "Grounded" is an architectural term, highlighting the importance of the foundation in establishing a firm base for a long-lasting structure. Paul employs the same combination of metaphors in his Letter to the Colossians as he exhorts, "Continue to live your lives in him, rooted and built up in him and established in the faith, just as you were taught," underlining the imperative for spiritual growth (Col 2:6–7).

The reality of spiritual maturity is shaped by Paul's understanding of the living Christ, who dwells within the life of the believer. The apostle emphasizes this indwelling through the language of being "in Christ," which he articulates in the phrase, "that Christ may dwell in your hearts through faith" (Eph 3:17). This amazing affirmation announces that Christ inhabits, energizes, and enables us to follow as his disciples. Such a dynamic affirms that ours is not a long-distance relationship with God but an intimate indwelling of the Spirit of Jesus, who urges us to hear and pay attention to his enlivening presence. The reciprocal dimension of the divine equation

---

6. Gutiérrez, *On Job*, 91–92.

7. See Donelson, *Colossians, Ephesians*, 83.

is that we live "within Christ," as Paul noted previously in the letter, where he described us as "seated [us] with him in the heavenly places in Christ Jesus" (2:6) and that "we are created in Christ Jesus for good works" (2:10). The union of being "in Christ" speaks to the mystery, explored in the previous chapter, that our lives contain overtones that surpass anything that our minds can contemplate or imagine. In spite of our spiritually myopic perspective, we do not live insignificant, unimportant lives; rather, we participate in the great renovation of humankind and the cosmos through our involvement in the new humanity found in Christ.

The observation that we are invited to strengthen our spiritual muscles reinforces Jesus' invitation to become his disciples (Matt 28:19). The word *mathētēs*, or "disciple," is related to the verb *manthanō*, or "to learn," which encourages us to become "learners" of Christ.[8] Going to "the school of Christ," as coined in the writings of Andrew Murray, involves an ongoing tutelage that takes place throughout the entire life journey.[9] It is an upward climb that continues through all phases of life and speaks to the whole person—heart, mind, and spirit. To this point our minds are to be completely renovated in Jesus through the reading and study of the Scriptures. By this ongoing immersion the word of God percolates up from the depths of our unconscious and reforms our conscious minds. This process, in turn, impacts our values, decisions, and choices. Commensurately, the word of God penetrates our hearts, considered the center of the will in the tradition of Judaism.[10] Jesus reinforces this understanding as he teaches his disciples that it is out of "the abundance of the heart" that good and evil flow (Luke 6:45). It is not surprising, then, that Paul implores in his prayer of intercession that our hearts be touched by the renovating power of God (Eph 3:16–17). Furthermore, we observe Paul's sensitivity to the work of the Spirit. When the apostle writes, "that you may be strengthened in your inner being through his Spirit" (3:16), he is emphasizing the role of the one who empowers our minds, hearts, and spirits to be responsive to Jesus in a deeper way. It is essential for this ongoing spiritual work to take place if we are to become fully aware of what Abba is able to accomplish as he "opens the eyes of our hearts" (1:18).

Being strengthened in Christ highlights the importance of the spiritual disciplines and their role for fruitful discipleship. The obvious discipline at hand is prayer, one that Paul models in the present context. This is his

---

8. *NIDNTT*, 1:483.
9. See Murray, *With Christ in the School of Prayer*.
10. *NIDNTT*, 2:181.

second extended intercession for the Ephesian community, revealing how critical prayer is in his pastoral perspective. As Paul demonstrates, prayer—or "prayers," as coined by the evangelist Luke (Acts 2:42)—is a lively conversation with Abba about all of life's concerns. There is nothing that lies outside of its domain.[11] As a result, we are invited to be transparent and vulnerable before our God so that the Holy Spirit can impress us with his presence and assuage our anxieties. The supporting discipline, of course, is the reading and study of the Scriptures, which nurtures our spiritual formation. This combination has been a long-standing practice in Protestant spirituality with its signature touchstone of *sola scriptura*. In the particular practice of *lectio divina*, a contemplative meditation of the sacred text, we bring together the two disciplines in a natural and nourishing way. *Lectio divina* is a liberating experience of praying the Scriptures.

Two writers on spirituality offer further practical suggestions to spur us on in our desire to see St. Paul's prayer realized—that we be "strengthened in our inner being with power"; that "Christ dwells in our hearts through faith"; that we are "rooted and grounded in love." In the exploration of the disciplines, the spiritual director and writer Evelyn Underhill advises that every believer has the responsibility to identify the spiritual exercises most helpful for him or her as an individual "learner" of Jesus. Even as we need physical exercise to gain muscle strength, so we need spiritual exercise to engender spiritual growth. Her salient point is that each learner does not necessarily include the same components in her or his spiritual regimen.[12] For example, one individual may find meditation to be an essential aspect for spiritual growth; another finds participation in a small group helpful; someone else is supported by attending a monthly spiritual retreat. The key is to discover the path for our own spiritual fruitfulness and to follow it with enthusiasm and stick-to-itiveness. To this end, Edward Farrell encourages us to be proactive in our desire to know Abba more and to persist in our spiritual work: "God is apprehended only if there be action and response on our part. It demands time and patience, patience with ourselves, a waiting for God. It is not a moment, but a cumulative process. Each day we must come to Him, and wait, allowing Him slowly to deposit His presence in us."[13]

---

11. See also Davey, *Abba's Whisper*, 46–57, for a broader discussion on the different types of prayer useful for spiritual growth.

12. Underhill, *Concerning the Inner Life*, 39.

13. Farrell, *Surprised by the Spirit*, 31.

Knowing God's Love

As an orchestra builds to a great crescendo, so Paul moves towards the climax of his prayer by inviting his readers to grasp the exhilarating promises of God by "comprehend[ing], with all the saints, what is the breadth and length and height and depth" of God's abundance found in Jesus Christ (Eph 3:18). The specific blessing Paul highlights is Jesus' amazing love: "and to know the love of Christ that surpasses knowledge, so that you may be filled with all the fullness of God" (3:19). To reinforce his point Paul highlights the word *gnōsis*, "to know," used two times in the phrases "to know the love" and "that surpasses knowledge" (3:19), which speaks of both an intellectual comprehension and an experiential learning of Christ's love. It is similar to the cry of Job when he utters before God, "I once knew you only by hearsay, now my eyes have seen you" (Job 42:5). Gutiérrez observes in his work on the ancient Old Testament figure, "Job now perceives that there is another way of knowing and speaking about God. His previous contact with God had been indirect, 'by hearsay' through others (his friends, for example); now it is direct, unmediated."[14] As a result, Job moves beyond mere knowledge to having a face-to-face encounter with God. It is this direct experience of divine love that Paul encourages his readers to inhabit. Such a love inundates the believer with "all the fullness of God" (Eph 3:19), because when all is said and done the greatest force in the universe is God's love (1 Cor 13:13). The invitation is to open up our hands and receive the gift of Abba's first love, for it is only his love that ultimately assuages the longing of the human heart. The knowledge of this first love speaks to both head and heart. It is both a knowledge that plumbs the depths of our intellectual capacity and a wisdom to be revealed in the actions of everyday living.

By embracing his love we are invited to incarnate Christ in the warp and woof of our lives and to do so in a spirit and practice of loving God and our neighbor. In the neighborhood of our own church, an Islamic community was targeted by an individual who started a fire on the roof of their mosque. Hearing of the vandalism, our leadership team decided to give the Islamic community a money gift as a sign of solidarity in standing against discrimination and to aid in the needed repairs. When I informed the church family of our intentions I was delighted to receive spontaneous donations from our congregants to complement the initial love gift. For me, this spontaneous act of kindness was a lovely expression of compassion

---

14. Gutiérrez, *On Job*, 85.

from one faith community to another who live and work in the same neighborhood. It was a gift ventured in good faith communicating the power of love for overcoming barriers and promoting God's shalom.

In a similar spirit we are invited to incarnate Jesus' love within the body of our own faith communities. The church is comprised of broken people who need forgiveness, patience, long-suffering, and acts of kindness. Ironically, in some ways it is more challenging to demonstrate compassion within the community than without, because we have higher expectations of each other and tend to be judgmental of one another. It is hard to let go when we feel judged or misunderstood by a fellow believer or when we observe other Christians acting in ways that counter the message of Christ. "Every person needs more love than he or she deserves," observes the German philosopher Jörg Splett, and nowhere is this more evident than in the church![15] This insight describes the human condition, and human beings make up the church. Both my sister and brother who have wounded me, and I who have wounded others need to experience this forgiving, restorative love. When we radiate such love, the community experiences reconciliation. *Shalom* fills up the crevices that separate us and creates a reservoir of acceptance.

As we do so, we begin to penetrate the mystery of Abba's love, which is destined to win the day by transforming human society into a human-divine paradigm of reciprocal love. No more will the Earth be ruled by egoistic self-interest, but it will be fully renovated by Abba's agape love demonstrated through the reign of his abundant lovingkindness and endless peace. Indeed, God's love is like a mighty river which is long, high, deep, and wide, enticing us to plunge in and immerse ourselves in its renewing and healing powers. May we say yes and engage Christ's primary love, as Paul opines, "Reach out and experience the breadth! Test its length! Plumb the depths! Rise to the heights! Live full lives, full in their fullness of God" (Eph 3:18–19 The Message).[16]

Comforted by God

In a spirit of joy Paul concludes his prayer with a rousing doxology: "Now to him who by the power at work within us is able to accomplish abundantly far more than all we can ask or imagine" (Eph 3:20). His note of

---

15. Breemen, *God Who Won't Let Go*, 21.
16. Peterson, *The Message*, Eph 3:18–19 (p. 480).

enthusiasm is based upon the divine power which shapes us over time into artistic masterpieces which manifest God's healing light to the world (2:10). It is a power, or *dynamis* (from which we derive the word "dynamite"), that expresses the Spirit's transformative work, which transcends our collective imagination, intellectual musings, and emotional longings. To punctuate this expression of praise, Paul employs the unusual word *hyperekperissou*, "accomplish abundantly," used only used twice in the New Testament, to sum up God's great work in Jesus Christ that surpasses our limited spiritual understanding.[17] Donelson suggests that by highlighting the Spirit's indwelling power the chained apostle wants to encourage and comfort the Ephesians as they live out their faith in a hostile environment.[18] God is on their side and his church will be victorious in spite of its humble beginnings and the apparent domination of the Roman Empire.

The prayer draws to a close with a benediction emphasizing God's eternal work located in Christ and manifested through his church: "To him be glory in the church and in Christ Jesus to all generations for ever and ever. Amen" (3:21). As we pause and carefully consider these words we note that the ecclesial blessing rings true for each and every generation of the body of Christ. We have legitimate concerns regarding the state of the contemporary church but God continues to work in and through it in spite of its spiritual disorder. Not only is it meant to be a word of solace which sustains us amidst the exigencies of life; it also acts as a harbinger for vibrant possibilities for faithful living. Paul reminds us that God does "far more than all we can ask or imagine" (3:20), which underlines the truth that Abba provides the resources for funding those imaginings for us. As a result, we are invited to embrace a mindset that is alert to God's creative work in our everyday. Christ who lives within us is greater than any force that stands against us, so we are able to proceed in confidence that new opportunities lie before us in Abba's name. In proclaiming the Beatitudes, Jesus demonstrates this hearty enthusiasm with the words "we are blessed," or "we are happy," and then announces the energizing outcomes that "we will inherit the earth," "we will be filled," "we will receive mercy," "we will see God," and "we will be named as his children" (Matt 5:1–11). These expressions speak not only to future hope but to our present condition in Christ as we say yes to an authentic relationship with the Divine Family.

---

17. The NIV translates it as "immeasurably more"; the Jerusalem Bible "infinitely more"; the KJV "exceedingly abundantly."

18. Donelson, *Colossians, Ephesians*, 84.

Through my teaching at Tyndale in Toronto and the seminaries in Cochabamba, Sucre, and Oruro, Bolivia, I am continually amazed at the potent ministry capacity that students both carry and live out. Mahatma Gandhi reminds us that "a single candle of light overcomes the darkness" and that "the love of one person is sufficient to compensate for the hatred of millions."[19] If so, how much more the energy from a nuclear explosion released through youthful minds and dynamic, committed spirits? I ask my students and parishioners, "What is Abba's dream for you?," "What possibilities does your life hold at this point in your journey?" These questions open up fertile reflection as we consider the impact of Abba's creative imagination for his people and as we pray over the potentialities that bubble up through our own meditation. Regardless of the limitations we frequently carry due to the difficulties of life, we are encouraged to receive and live out our present day, for it is *the day* which connects us with Abba's infinite love.

The heart of being a Christian is to know the love of God. It is the joy of knowing Abba's first love that draws us to him and sustains us amidst life's trials. We belong to him and he will never forsake us, for his love is truly bottomless. As van Breemen celebrates,

> No matter how deeply we are immersed in God's love, we never reach the bottom, since that does not exist. God's love has no limit, no end. Trying to imagine this we become dizzy. Our imagination is too limited . . . God's love is unlimited, bottomless, without any boundary. It is sheer surprise.[20]

It is this crazy love that penetrates deep into Paul's psyche, transforming him from being an angry, self-righteous person who could not see beyond the biases of his own group into a loving soul who values every person regardless of clan or tribe (Eph 3:14). This life-giving love flows from the heart of God and comes to us through Jesus, as the Scriptures declare, "God's love was revealed among us in this way: God sent his only Son into the world so that we might live through him. In this is love, not that we loved God but that he loved us and sent his Son to be the atoning sacrifice for our sins" (1 John 4:9–10). Our *raison d'être* is located in Abba's bottomless love and through it he draws us into a place of intimacy as his passionate bride. It is his desire that we accept his love and reciprocate by loving him and our neighbor so that the world moves towards wholeness and love reigns

---

19. Farrell, *Beams of Prayer*, 78.
20. Breemen, *God Who Won't Let Go*, 28–29.

in every corner of his creation. Our own expression of this charity begins where we find ourselves—in our immediate relationships and in our own faith community, where opportunities abound for revealing the self-giving love of the Divine Family.

Questions for Reflection

1. It is so reassuring that "we belong to God." We are his sons and daughters and nothing can nullify the reality of this deep-seated relationship. In the coming week during your prayers repeat the phrase "I belong to God" and allow it to flow deep into your consciousness. Hold on to this truth amidst the challenges which are bound to come your way.

2. In Paul's prayer we are encouraged to strengthen our relationship with Abba. We are invited to take responsibility for our Christian growth and not simply coast along in our spiritual dynamic. Think about how you can intentionally spend time with Christ and grow your spiritual muscles even as you might design a physical exercise regimen. Write in your journal your plan to seek after Jesus this week. What specific exercises will you engage to make it happen?

3. "Everyone needs more love than he or she deserves." In light of this truth imagine walking with Jesus and hearing him tell you that he loves you and that you have a special place in his heart. How does that make you feel? What is your response to Jesus?

4. Paul ends his prayer to the Ephesians with a word of comfort as he declares, "Now to him who by the power at work within us is able to accomplish abundantly more than all we can ask or imagine." It is a word of reassurance reminding us that no matter what problem we face, Abba is greater and he will bring us safely through to the other side. Spend a few moments reflecting on God's amazing grace and praise him for his bottomless love.

7

Grown Up Christians

Ephesians 4:1–16

"We are all called to do, not extraordinary things, but very ordinary things, with an extraordinary love that flows from the heart of God . . . Love is communion, communion with God and with our brothers and sisters. Love is manifested in all the little things of life that build community, not in heroic acts."

Jean Vanier, Community and Growth

"*I therefore, the prisoner in the Lord,*
> *beg you to lead a life worthy of the calling to which you have been called,*
> *with all humility and gentleness, with patience, bearing with one another in love,*
>> *making every effort to maintain the unity of the Spirit in the bond of peace.*

There is one body and one Spirit,
> *just as you were called to the one hope of your calling,*
> *one Lord, one faith, one baptism, one God and Father of all,*
>> *who is above all and through all and in all.*

But each of us was given grace according to the measure of Christ's gift.

Therefore it is said, 'When he ascended on high he made captivity itself a captive;
> *he gave gifts to his people.'*
(When it says, 'He ascended,' what does it mean but that he had also descended into the lower parts of the earth?
He who descended is the same one who ascended far above all the heavens,
> *so that he might fill all things.)*

The gifts he gave were that some would be apostles, some prophets, some evangelists, some pastors and teachers, to equip the saints for the work of ministry,
> *for building up the body of Christ,*
>> *until all of us come to the unity of the faith and of the knowledge of the Son of God,*
>> *to maturity, to the measure of the full stature of Christ.*

We must no longer be children, tossed to and fro and blown about by every wind of doctrine,
> *by people's trickery, by their craftiness in deceitful scheming.*

But speaking the truth in love, we must grow up in every way
> *into him who is the head, into Christ,*
> *from whom the whole body, joined and knitted together by every ligament with which it is equipped,*
> *as each part is working properly, promotes the body's growth*
>> *in building itself up in love."*   *(Ephesians 4:1–16)*

Henri Nouwen tells the story of his enthusiastic trips to the circus to take in the excitement, the different performing acts, and especially the acrobatic troupe "The Flying Rodleighs."[1] Whenever the Rodleighs came to town, he took residents from the L'Arche community Daybreak to enjoy their entertaining high-wire tumbling feats. He viewed the trapeze artists as a harmonious team who only experienced success as they worked together as a finely tuned machine. It was not about one person, even if it was the artist flying across the ring, but about the intricacies of teamwork.

---

1. Gateway Films, *Henri Nouwen*. See also Nouwen, *Our Greatest Gift*, 66–67.

The flyer and the catcher had to work as one to avert disaster and successfully complete the routine. Furthermore, the most important person of the duo was not the flyer, whom the crowd enthusiastically applauded, but the catcher who grasped the flyer and kept her safe.

Nouwen sees this intricate synergy as a metaphor of how humanity has the capacity for creative and peaceful living. The troupe demonstrates how people can live together in harmony, valuing the abilities of each person and releasing each of them to make his or her specific contribution. I suggest that Nouwen's observations apply in our understanding of the church: as the teamwork of the Flying Rodleighs is a metaphor for humanity in creative partnership, so the circus troupe demonstrates how the church can live harmoniously while celebrating the value and gifts of each member. As the flyer and catcher work in tandem, so Abba invites us to fly and boldly live our lives with the confidence that he is the Catcher who keeps us from falling. It is this powerful interconnection of the body of Christ and the assurance that Abba is working in our midst that Paul develops in the pastoral application that comprises the second half of his Letter to the Ephesians.

The Primacy of Our Calling

Paul begins this unit by reminding the Ephesians of his own calling and the cost he willingly pays while sitting in a jail cell for the sake of the gospel. He is indeed a "prisoner in the Lord" due to his inveterate commitment to bring the message of Christ to the Gentile community (Eph 4:1). His own sense of vocation leads him to encourage the faith community to live out their own calling with purpose and passion. He exhorts the church to grasp hold of "the calling to which you have been called" (4:1) and instructs them to maintain unity "as you were called to the one hope of your calling" (4:4). By employing a fourfold repetition of the word "calling, " or *klēsis* (4:2, 4), Paul highlights the significance of knowing and following Christ in an obedient and diligent manner. As he reminds the community "to lead a life worthy of the calling" (4:1), he underlines the importance of developing "an everyday mind" that keeps Jesus as the fulcrum of their daily decision-making process. Karl Rahner notes, "It's evident that routine is not just a part of my life, not even just the greatest part, but the whole. Every day is 'everyday.' Everything I do is routine, because everything can rob me of the one and only thing I really need, which is You, my God."[2]

2. Rahner, *Encounters with Silence*, 49.

The fruit of such a lifestyle is demonstrated in the virtues Paul enumerates, reflecting the characteristics of Christ: humility, gentleness, patience, and bearing with one another in love. These are shown by Jesus as he made his triumphal entry into Jerusalem, as prophesied by Zechariah, "Tell the daughter of Zion, Look, your king is coming to you, humble [meek, gentle], and mounted on a donkey, and on a colt, the foal of a donkey" (Matt 21:5), and praised in the Beatitudes, "Blessed are the meek [gentle], for they will inherit the earth" (Matt 5:5). Our calling to know Christ and to be his light in the world is played out through a similar lifestyle marked by compassion, respect, and enduring love, even towards those who hold contrary positions.[3] This fundamental calling is to become our primary vocation in life, transcending career choices, success, earning power, social accolades, or any other personal aspirations.

We need to underscore our calling because of our inherent attraction to and engagement with the mores of the world. The apostle John understands this propensity to attachment as he writes, "Do not love the world or the things in the world. The love of the Father is not in those who love the world; for all that is in the world—the desire of the flesh, the desire of the eyes, the pride in riches—comes not from the Father but from the world" (1 John 2:15–16). In this word of caution John is not deriding the natural world but humanity's decision to live apart from God and seek fulfillment in the things of creation. Such a perspective reinforces the false self, perpetuated by one's ego seeking prominence over others, driven by a deep commitment to competition and comparison. In contrast to the world's values, Paul promotes the life-enhancing pattern of Christ, "bearing with one another in love" (Eph 4:2). It is instructive to note that the word "bearing," or *anechō*, has the sense of "enduring, bearing with" or "patiently suffering" the idiosyncrasies of others in an attitude of sacrificial love, as Paul urges in a well-known passage, "Love is patient; love is kind . . . it is not irritable or resentful . . . it bears all things" (1 Cor 13:4–7).[4] Together we lament that such a loving perspective is often a challenge to maintain. For this reason, Paul insists on upholding a lively devotion to our higher calling of "knowing Christ" (Phil 3:10) so that our great yes to Abba is not usurped by secondary or competing desires.

---

3. Capon, *Kingdom, Grace, Judgment*, 19.
4. *NIDNTT*, 2:765–67.

Unity as a Core Value

The good news is that leading a life "worthy of the calling" is not a solo effort; rather, we are invited to pursue our calling together. Paul makes this point to the Ephesian community highlighting the intentional energy required in walking together. "Make every effort to maintain the unity of the Spirit," he urges them (Eph 4:3). Indeed, the verb *spoudazō*, or "make every effort," can be translated "be zealous," "eager," "hasten," all implying an intentional act of the will in seeking peace.[5] We are encouraged to help one another move towards Christ and not become blocks that get in the way of other people's growth. For this reason, Paul comments upon the unity that we intrinsically share in Christ through a creedal statement: "There is one body and one Spirit, just as you were called to the one hope of your calling, one Lord, one faith, one baptism, one God and Father of all, who is above all and through all and in all" (4: 4–6). The sevenfold repetition of our oneness recapitulates the truth that we are on the journey of faith together and it is essential that we make the commensurate effort to fulfill our calling.

The challenge we face is that we become so accustomed to disunity that we accept it as the norm. Disharmony is the tenor of our age! It pervades the spheres of politics, socioeconomics, and ecclesiastical affairs, thus penetrating our understanding and practice within the life of the church. It is so easy for us to act in a divisive manner; it is second nature for us! We need an active remembering of Paul's cogent appeal for unity. We must not allow our own desire "to be right" to trump our commitment for maintaining the peace of Christ (4:3).

A practical demonstration of Paul's admonition for ecclesiastical unity was his entreaty for the collection of monies to support the impoverished church in Jerusalem.[6] Wherever the apostle traveled in his missionary journeys he encouraged the local churches to make monetary sacrifices for the good of the Jerusalem church.[7] Evidently, this was no easy task, as the Gentile assemblies more often than not had limited resources themselves and the mother church was a long distance away and unknown to the Asian and Greek communities. Nevertheless, for Paul the collection became a symbol for the unity of the church in its manifestation as the body of Christ.

---

5. Kubo, *Reader's Greek-English Lexicon*, 184.
6. See Wright, *Paul*, 167.
7. See 2 Cor 8–9; Rom 15:22–29.

Similarly, in our own day, sacrificial giving is a significant expression of incarnating the presence of Jesus. Where and how we deal with our finances is a telling sign of our commitment in following Christ. Money is such a central factor in our everyday lives that a willingness to give it away for the cause of Christ is an indication of one's heartfelt discipleship. From my work in Bolivia, I have also seen prayer and worship supporting the act of giving grow a sense of unity between varying faith communities. Differences of doctrine, language, and cultural traditions give way to the shared exercise of prayer, praise, and sacrificial giving for the work of God's kingdom. I have seen heated arguments over competing ideas evolve into joyful worship as groups come together through prayer and rally around a common goal expressed through sacrificial giving.

Paul's admonition "to make every effort to maintain the unity of the Spirit" (Eph 4:3) continues to ring loudly as it speaks to the fundamental harmony within the Divine Family and our call for imitating God within the dynamic of church life. As the Celtic cross presents the persons of the Trinity flowing sympathetically within the Godhead, so we are entreated to weave in and out of each other's lives in a spirit of peace (4:3). The fathers and mothers of the early church referred to such a respectful movement as "docility"—an irenic spirit in which individuals are encouraged to be open and willing to learn from the teaching of others rather than simply reacting to contrary beliefs.[8] Such gentleness is based on a high level of respect when community members are slow to critique one another and attempt to find points of connection between competing perspectives. It is precisely on this point that Jesus takes issue with the Pharisees and Sadducees, who deeply hold positions of judgment and critique and lack any significant expression of docility.[9]

Within the argumentative discourse of our day an elevated appreciation of docility would go a long way in calming the divisive spirit that pervades much of the contemporary church. Roberta Bondi in her work *To Pray and Love* cautions us on our propensity for judging one another and the negative effects it has on both our lives and the communities we represent:

> Judgmentalism destroys community; it destroys those who do the judging, and, even more seriously for the monastic teachers, it often destroys (and certainly excludes from community) the one who is judged. On a small scale judgmentalism destroys

---

8. Smith, "Virtue of Docility."
9. See Matt 6:5–6; 9:10–13; 15:1–20; ch. 23.

marriages, families, and churches. On a wider scale it provides the major fuel of racism, sexism, neglect of the poor, and national self-righteousness.[10]

When we recognize the powerful impact of judgmentalism, we see how essential Paul's exhortation is. It is not simply an attractive but unattainable objective; rather, it is a core value for any Christian community. We must eagerly pursue unity in the dynamics of the local assembly.

Unity Expressed in Diversity

Paul does not describe a monochromatic unity but one which is characterized by a diversity of colors, talents, and expressions. This vibrant montage is aptly presented as each member of the church is uniquely gifted by Christ (Eph 4:7). The apostle indicates this outpouring of spiritual gifts as he quotes a psalm text, "When he ascended on high he made captivity itself a captive; he gave gifts to his people" (4:8), followed by an explanation that Christ is the one who descended and ascended and is now distributing gifts to his people (4:8–10). The reference to "descending and ascending" is understood by commentators in various ways but is perhaps most clearly interpreted as a reference to Christ's incarnation, resurrection, ascension, and subsequent giving of spiritual gifts through the Holy Spirit.[11]

Subsequently, Paul identifies a number of these spiritual gifts, including apostles, prophets, evangelists, pastors, and teachers (4:11); elsewhere he suggests an expanded array of gifts involving exhortation, giving, leading, and compassion (Rom 12:6–8), and healing, working of miracles, discernment of spirits, tongues, and interpretation of tongues (1 Cor 12: 4–11). Paul states that the purpose of these gifts is "to equip the saints for the work of ministry, for building up the body of Christ, until all of us come to the unity of the faith and of the knowledge of the Son of God" (Eph 4:12–13). This affirmation becomes a foundational strategy for expressing the collective nature of the body of Christ, where each believer is gifted and plays an important part in the ongoing spiritual health of the community. Christ has gifted us and he has done so for the purpose of building up of his new society, the people of God. Hence, it is imperative that we embrace our giftedness and complete the good works he has set out for us to fulfill

---

10. Bondi, *To Pray and Love*, 109.
11. See Martin, *Ephesians*, 50–51; Stott, *God's New Society*, 159.

(2:10). In doing so we assume the role the Scriptures announce of becoming his priests who "proclaim the mighty acts of him who called us out of darkness and into his marvelous light" (1 Pet 2:9).

The description of a gifted community with a "parity of membership" is a significant departure from "the highly structured patterns of the Greco-Roman society," the commentator Cousar points out, and provides a powerful dynamic for the formation of the new humanity.[12] Paul envisions an entirely new society—one which transcends the cultural barriers of the first century: divisions between competing ethnic groups, between slave owners and slaves, between patrons and laborers, between men and women, between Jews and Gentiles.[13] Through this groundbreaking development believers from every part of the socioeconomic demographic are gifted by the same Christ and contribute to the spiritual life of the new community of God. The apostle not only affirms the importance of this transformative mélange but insists on its need for ensuring the health of the new *laos* of God.

Alas, the spiritual fruitfulness of diversity within the body of Christ is not fully appreciated in our own day, as homogeneous groupings are promoted and marketed as the way to achieve church growth. As evidenced throughout Ephesians, sacrificing diversity to create a homogeneous community results in the establishment of a distorted church which imitates the mores of the old humanity rather than following the revolutionary Spirit of the new humanity of God.

The paradigm of unity and diversity is made clear in Paul's metaphor for the church as the "body of Christ." Looking back at earlier sections of the Ephesians letter, we observe a number of references for the church: "made him the head over all things for the church, which is his body" (1:22–23); "creat[ing] in himself one new humanity in place of the two . . . reconcil[ing] both groups to God in one body" (2:16); "the Gentiles have become fellow-heirs, members of the same body" (3:6). The language surfaces again in our present unit when Paul describes the church's "oneness—"i.e., "one body" (4:4)—and connects it with diversity as he comments upon the impact of the spiritual gifts for the "building up the body of Christ" (4:16). Body language is filled out with additional references to "the whole body" being "joined and knitted together" and the "body's growth" being "built up in love" (4:16). Through this collective tableau Paul presents the church as a living, pulsating human body with Christ as the "head" (4:15) and "the

---

12. Cousar, *Letters of Paul*, 142.
13. Cousar, *Letters of Paul*, 142.

people of God" as his "ligaments" doing the work of ministry. This image is a dynamic representation of a passionate people.

Unfortunately, the picture is sadly undermined when we view the church as an institution rather than the spirited body of Christ. Furthermore, it is counterproductive when believers minimize the importance of the church or perceive it to be an archaic institution with little relevance for one's faith journey or even an impediment to a true experience of God. Eugene Peterson recognizes this enervating outlook and cautions the contemporary church on its shortcomings:

> We are ardent after God but cool towards the church. It is not irreligion or indifference that keeps many away from the church, but just the opposite: the church is perceived and experienced as a carcinogenic pollutant in the pure air of religion. Many people, wanting to nurture faith in God, instead of entering a company of saints who still look and act a lot more like sinners, take a long walk on an ocean beach, or hike a high mountain, or immerse themselves in Dostoyevsky or Stravinsky or Georgia O'Keeffe.[14]

Peterson's point is that such a position may lower one's blood pressure but does not necessarily contribute to the work of God on planet Earth or provide the communal environment which is indispensable for spiritual vitality.

We need to hear again and again the profound truth that the church is not an organization, but an organism; not a corporation, but a community; not a business, but the enlivened body of the living Christ.[15] Christ is both "gift" and "the Giver of gifts," and desires that we become his skilled stewards in the formation of the new humanity. Receiving our mandate, it is imperative that we reclaim our vision of being the "body of Christ" on planet Earth. We have a mission to fulfill and the church of Christ has a central role to play in the accomplishment of God's purposes. The apostle insists upon a communal journey of faith in opposition to a solitary path and lays this out as he portrays the way forward to spiritual maturity.

---

14. Peterson, *Reversed Thunder*, 44–45.

15. 1 Cor 12:4–11; Rom 12:5–8; Eph 4:1–16. See Snyder, *Community of the King*, 57.

The Invitation to Maturity

The synthesis of unity and diversity moves us towards our goal of maturity in Christ. To this end the apostle piles up a series of words which lead us in the direction of spiritual fullness: "come to" or "attain," "knowledge of the Son," "to maturity," "to the measure of the full stature" (Eph 4:13), "no longer be children" (4:14), "grow up in every way into him who is the head" (4:15). These expressions of Paul call us to pursue the path of spiritual growth. He recognizes that conversion is not simply a one-time event but a continual turning to God. We are on an incredible journey to become like Christ—to grow up into the likeness of "our head, into Christ" (4:15). Van Breemen calls this process an "ongoing reorientation towards God" which results in a "new pattern" of "actions and reactions."[16] Peterson is even more blunt in his understanding of the process: "There is a relentless quality to the word of God that insists that we face up to our sloth, our pride, our avarice—all the things that separate us from God's complete victory in us, every part that is diseased or immature, that defeats our joy or interferes with another's salvation."[17] C. S. Lewis, in his unique sense of drama, adds force to this commitment to the process of spiritual growth. He hearkens back to the demanding and seemingly impossible command of Jesus in the Beatitudes to "be perfect" (Matt 5:48):

> The command *Be ye perfect* is not idealistic gas. Nor is it a command to do the impossible. He is going to make us into creatures that can obey that command. He said (in the Bible) that we were 'gods' and He is going to make good His words. If we let Him—for we can prevent Him, if we choose—He will make the feeblest and filthiest of us into a god or goddess, a dazzling, radiant, immortal creature, pulsating all through with such energy and joy and wisdom and love as we cannot now imagine, a bright stainless mirror which reflects back to God perfectly (though, of course, on a smaller scale) His own boundless power and delight and goodness. The process will be long and in parts be very painful, but that is what we are in for. Nothing less. He meant what He said.[18]

While Lewis emphasizes here the role that God plays in our spiritual maturity, he nevertheless assumes our partnership in the process as St. Paul outlines in his admonitions in Ephesians 4.

---

16. Breemen, *Let All God's Glory Through*, 23.
17. Peterson, *Reversed Thunder*, 53.
18. Lewis, *Mere Christianity*, 205–6.

Again, this is not a singular path. We travel together as the people of God and do so in the bonds of community. As we have seen, Paul's use of the metaphor of the church as a body, with each of us as ligaments working together under the leadership of Christ our head, affirms this shared commitment. Every believer has their own part to play for the effectual working of the body. We are all called to participate and use our gifts for the work of the kingdom, and as we do so we mutually benefit by receiving life from the other members of Christ's body.

The ultimate expression of spiritual maturity is the manifestation of love. Paul works towards this affirmation with the conclusion that the body "works properly as it promotes the body's growth in building itself up in love" (Eph 4:16). Love is the greatest virtue and is the pinnacle of Abba's presence within our individual faith journey as well as our collective one. We are only able to sustain this loving path as we are confident that Abba holds us firmly in his arms of love. Without his first love we are not able to continue on the road of sacrificial self-giving. Thomas Merton understands this reality: "The root of Christian love is not the will to love, but *the faith that one is loved*. The faith that one is loved *by God*. That faith that one is loved by God although unworthy—or, rather, irrespective of one's worth!"[19]

Fuelled by God's limitless love, we are energized by the indwelling Holy Spirit to love our sisters and brothers in Christ and our neighbor as ourselves. We recognize, of course, that this ability to love others does not mean that we find everyone likeable; individuals may still be irascible, irritating, and uninteresting! Yet, as an action of the will we are able to make loving choices that desire the best for the other person and truly work for their well-being. Certainly, it is this characteristic of agape love that is to shape the spirit of Christ's church and becomes the harbinger of a renovated world that manifests the love of the Creator.

A mature church, described as a body of love, is one characterized by growth. Paul emphasizes this point by combining the following phrases: "building up the body of Christ" (Eph 4:12), "the measure of the full stature of Christ" (4:13), "grow up in every way" (4:15), "as each part is working properly, promotes the body's growth" (4:16). These descriptions characterize a community that is energetic, vibrant, and organically flourishing. Growth is illustrated through the depiction of spiritual fruit and the exercising of spiritual gifts by the membership of the faith community. Paul details the fruitful nature of the spiritual life in his Letter to the Galatians

---

19. Merton, *New Seeds of Contemplation*, 75.

with the fruit of the Spirit: "love, joy, peace, patience, kindness, generosity, faithfulness, gentleness, and self-control" (Gal 5:22–23). Again, he also presents the body of Christ as a gifted membership where each believer has spiritual gifts and exercises their gifts for the edification of the faith community (Eph 4:12). These two criteria of fruitfulness and giftedness for the measure of spiritual maturity cannot be overemphasized.

We miss the mark when we define a flourishing church by categories of numerical growth, budget size, and extensive programs. Lamentably, we often focus on these tangential matters and identify them as the key elements of a healthy church! Howard Snyder recognizes this tendency and cautions the contemporary church on its unhelpful outcomes:

> There is too easy a tendency to build large local churches with the accompanying inevitable institutionalism, bureaucracy and emphasis on buildings. The subtle temptation to imitate secular institutional models such as government, industry and the university becomes over-whelming, and the church slips into institutionalism with the rigidity, impersonality and hierarchy that go along with the package.[20]

We never hear Paul complaining about a need for more money, renovated buildings, or innovative programming. Instead, he encourages the formation of a participative, inclusionary community enthusiastic for God's work, the imitation of Christ, and the engagement of their spiritual gifts for the kingdom of heaven.

The Spirituality of the Circle

Paul's use of the body metaphor is a way of addressing the organic nature of the local church. He refers to Christ as the "head of the church" (4:15) but this does not necessarily indicate that hierarchy is the designated model for the community of faith. As is pointed out elsewhere, "headship" (*kephalē*) often speaks to the "nature of source," which resonates well with the body metaphor.[21] Christ is the head of the church in terms of being its "source or spring" from which the rest of the body draws life. As a result, the body components link together and grow towards maturity as each part flourishes. The body metaphor evokes the image of a dance in which each dancer moves

---

20. Snyder, *Community of the King*, 123.
21. See Evans, *Woman in the Bible*, 65–66.

with grace and sensitivity, creating an artistic expression which transcends their singular efforts. Jean Vanier proposes the analogy of "the spirituality of the circle" to evoke a sensitive receptivity within communal life, "rooted in the everyday . . . the spirituality of Nazareth . . . [implying] littleness, love of little things and humility."[22] Through this image Vanier advocates the development of a lively community that exhibits a continual weaving in and out of each other's lives, where leadership is expressed from a diversification of sources depending on the specific needs.

In contrast, the hierarchical paradigm which focuses on organizational flow charts and top-down decision-making has limited effectiveness in serving the contemporary church. As Paul argues, the collective membership of the faith community represents the body of Christ and not simply a few talented individuals. The apostle demonstrates this integrated network by identifying the variety of spiritual gifts mentioned earlier. Every member is invited to express their gifts in a manner that is fluid and organic as is needed in the body of Christ. As Paul advocates, "To each is given the manifestation of the Spirit for the common good," and again, "All these are activated by one and the same Spirit, who allots to each one individually just as the Spirit chooses" (1 Cor 12:7, 11).

In the Corinthian correspondence Paul describes this paradigm in action: "What should be done then my friends? When you come together, each one has a hymn, a lesson, a revelation, a tongue, or an interpretation. Let all things be done for building up" (1 Cor 14:26). This is not meant to be an exclusionary template for worship gatherings but is instructive on how spiritual gifts are deployed for the building up of the people of God. In light of the apostle's description of body life it seems that an inflexible system of hierarchical control hinders the spontaneous movement of the Spirit vital for a healthy community. As a result, we can be left with a truncated congregation where a multitude of spiritual gifts are unexpressed and unappreciated and a select few (often the paid clergy) express their spiritual gifts.

For the circle model to be effective there must be a strong commitment to communal listening. Such attentiveness requires an investment of time, but it is worth the effort as individuals have time to understand the issues and contribute to the final outcomes. For a variety of reasons—a lack of patience, a commitment to efficiency, and a frustration with the hard work of paying attention—we often cut short the listening stage in the guise of effective management. We become so conditioned by our culture's

---

22. Vanier, *Community and Growth*, 302–3.

fascination for utility that our listening skills are diminished and the benefits that listening engenders are undermined.

Commensurate with attending to one another is the importance of listening for the whispers of Abba's voice. Such awareness is facilitated through both a spirit of prayer and a spirit of love, which serves as a mortar for binding the *laos* of God together. Paul calls for this demonstration of prayerful love as he highlights the virtues of humility, gentleness, and patience. He emphasizes the need to "bear with one another in love" and "maintain the unity of the Spirit in the bond of peace"—no easy combination of quiet activity to achieve (Eph 4:2–3). This tandem of love and prayer is revealed as one waits upon God and truly listens for his voice, as echoed by Isaiah's refrain, "Have ears that are awake" (Isa 50:4), and in Jesus' imperative, "Let anyone with ears to hear listen!" (Mark 4:9; Rev 2:7, 11). As we are mindful of Abba's voice and demonstrate "awakened ears," the discerning path is made clear and the community is able to move forward in confidence knowing that it understands the leading of the Spirit.

Together we embrace the synergy that comprises our unity in Christ and the diversity demonstrated through the giftedness of the Spirit. It is this symbiotic relationship that leads us deeper into spiritual maturity and empowers the church of Christ for effective ministry. In light of this essential pattern, it is important for us to consider our own participation in the body of Christ and the lively expression of our spiritual gifts. Are we committed to a local assembly and using our spiritual gifts for its betterment? Do we persevere amidst the challenges of communal life or give up due to the frustrations of interpersonal conflict? It is not sufficient to simply be members of a church family; instead, we are invited to actively engage in the dynamic interplay of the body of Christ, which represents the giftedness and compassionate presence of Jesus our Lord. As we affirm and exhibit a sincere desire to participate in the church of Christ we become his chosen instrument for advancing God's purposes in the world. It is to this end that we shout out our unwavering yes and unreservedly give ourselves to Christ as his passionate bride.

Questions for Reflection

1. Paul stresses the essential characteristic of unity in the church of Christ. Unfortunately, the broader church does not have a great record of maintaining unity, but instead demonstrates a propensity for

schisms. Why do you think this is the case? Can you identify practical steps the church might take to further the cause of unity?

2. As we have seen, there is a resplendent diversity of spiritual gifts within the body of Christ. Write down in your journal the nature of your own spiritual gifts and share these thoughts with a trusted friend to corroborate your understanding. In light of these insights, how are you able to engage your gifts for the benefit of the church?

3. The beauty of the body of Christ is that it moves in the direction of growth and spiritual fecundity. In what ways do you see this movement towards maturity being demonstrated in your community of faith? In your prayer times thank God for the spiritual growth that is evident in your church family and pray for the Spirit's continuing work in your midst.

4. Jesus invites us to listen deeply and attentively for his voice as we work together in the body of Christ. How would you evaluate your listening skills when it comes to spiritual formation? Are there some practical steps you can implement which will help you in the path towards qualitative listening? Make these adjustments in the coming weeks and see if they assist you in the listening process.

8

Embracing the True Self

Ephesians 4:17—5:2

"Every one of us is shadowed by an illusory person: a false self.

This is the man that I want myself to be but who cannot exist, because God does not know anything about him. And to be unknown of God is altogether too much privacy.

My false and private self is the one who wants to exist outside the reach of God's will and God's love—outside of reality and outside of life. And such a self cannot help but be an illusion.

We are not very good at recognizing illusions, least of all the ones we cherish about ourselves—the ones we are born with and which feed the roots of sin. For most of the people in the world, there is no greater subjective reality than the false self of theirs, which cannot exist. A life devoted to the cult of this shadow is what is called a life of sin."

THOMAS MERTON, *NEW SEEDS OF CONTEMPLATION*

"Now this I affirm and insist on in the Lord:
  you must no longer live as the Gentiles live, in the futility of their minds,
They are darkened in their understanding,
  alienated from the life of God because of their ignorance and hardness of heart.
They have lost all sensitivity and have abandoned themselves to licentiousness,
  greedy to practise every kind of impurity.

That is not the way you learned Christ!
For surely you have heard about him and were taught in him, as truth is in Jesus.
You were taught to put away your former way of life,
    your old self, corrupt and deluded by its lusts,
    and to be renewed in the spirit of your minds,
    and to clothe yourselves with the new self,
        created according to the likeness of God in true righteousness
        and holiness.

So then, putting away falsehood, let us all speak the truth to our neighbors,
    for we are members of one another.
Be angry but do not sin; do not let the sun go down on your anger,
    and do not make room for the devil.
Thieves must give up stealing;
    rather let them labour and work honestly with their own hands,
        so as to have something to share with the needy.
Let no evil talk come out of your mouths,
    but only what is useful for building up, as there is need,
        so that your words may give grace to those who hear.

And do not grieve the Holy Spirit of God,
    with which you were marked with a seal for the day of redemption.
Put away from you all bitterness and wrath and anger and wrangling
and slander,
    together with all malice,
and be kind to one another, tender-hearted, forgiving one another,
    as God in Christ has forgiven you.

Therefore be imitators of God, as beloved children,
    and live in love, as Christ loved us and gave himself up for us,
        a fragrant offering and sacrifice to God."
                            (Ephesians 4:17–5:2)

On occasion in his letters, St. Paul employs the image of an individual who takes off an old outfit and replaces it with a new one to illustrate a person who forsakes an ego-centered lifestyle and replaces it with a new life of selfless love. When we read his exhortation to "put away your former way of life, your old self . . . and be renewed in the spirit of your minds, and to clothe yourselves with the new self" (Eph 4:22–24), we imagine a once-for-all transformation from the old to the new self. In fact, the opposite is more accurate: the renovation of the human condition is a process that takes time, determination, and much grace. In saying this, we do not deny that there is an initial point of conversion which exhibits substantive change, but simply acknowledge the truth that the path of spiritual integration is a lifelong journey. We wish for a rapid and complete transformation, but in reality we typically face ongoing hurdles, disappointments, and failures even as we persevere in living a life of obedience and service.

Allow us to retell a parable which presents the inherent struggle we all face when it comes to spiritual growth.[1] The story begins with a scientist who has spent years developing a strain of a multicolored butterfly which surpasses the beauty of all others. As the day comes for the butterfly to emerge from its cocoon, he invites his friends and colleagues to gather around and celebrate the decisive moment. As planned, the butterfly starts the arduous task of chipping through the cocoon. Little by little the right wing emerges, then its body, but problematically the left wing remains partially attached to the cocoon. The butterfly vigorously flaps its free wing to free the toggled wing but is unsuccessful and lies exhausted due to its strenuous efforts. In desperation, the learned scientist cuts away a portion of the cocoon to free the entangled wing. The effort seems successful as the butterfly gathers its strength, pushes through the cavity, breaking free from the cocoon, and lies unattached on the laboratory table. Spontaneously the room breaks into applause, congratulating the scientist for his decisive and innovative work! However, after a few minutes the acclamation turns to subdued whispers as it becomes evident to all that the butterfly is unable to fly. The doctor's well-intentioned intervention actually impaired the butterfly's ability to fly, curtailing nature's way of forcing blood to the wing tips. What was perceived to be needless flailing about actually represented the supreme effort required to successfully exit the cocoon. Without the needed exertion the butterfly discarded the cocoon but never gained the ability to fly.

---

1. Keating, *Foundations for Centering Prayer*, 194–95.

God does not make the same mistake with us! We seek a quick and efficient process for spiritual renovation with a minimum of spiritual struggles. Our desire is for Abba to step in and make our lives all better, even as a young child wants comfort from her mother. But God wisely holds back his hand knowing that our transformation is inhibited if the process does not run its full course. Keating concludes his story by affirming the truth that Abba understands better than the scientist what is actually needed: "God holds back his infinite mercy from rushing to the rescue when we are in temptation and difficulties. He will not actively intervene because the struggle is opening and preparing every recess of our being for the divine energy of grace."[2] With this image in mind we return to Paul's exhortation concerning spiritual growth and consider the nature of the transformational journey towards the authentic self.

A Recognition of the False Self

Paul begins by recognizing the reality of the false and true self as he encourages his readers to "put away your former way of life, your old self" (Eph 4:22) and to "clothe yourselves with the new self, created according to the likeness of God" (4:24). The actual wording is *endyō*, or "to clothe yourself" (Eph 4:24; Col 3:10), *apekdyomai*, or "to strip off" (Col 3:9), and *apotithēmi*, or "to put off, lay aside" (Eph 4:22). The metaphor of taking off old clothes and putting on new clothes represents in an everyday way the radical transformation of moving from the false to the new self. For the apostle, the false self represents the person who is tied up in a created facade bandied about to make an impression on others. It is a world of the ego where one desires to be known, celebrated, and applauded—a world where one rises to the top and is perceived as important and having the first place. Such a worldview suggests we draw our strength through merit and by comparing ourselves with others in a game of competition. The glaring limitation is that we rarely occupy first place; we are surrounded by greater lights, so that our self-worth is overshadowed by our inveterate commitment to comparison. Ironically, this preoccupation with comparison hides the true self, which is created uniquely and loved deeply by the divine Trinity. Deep inside us is the true person, but it is wrapped up like an Egyptian mummy by our feeble efforts to impress others; as a result, its beauty is hidden.

2. Keating, *Foundations for Centering Prayer*, 196.

Parker Palmer illustrates this truth by reflecting upon the poet's question, "Ask me whether what I have done is my Life."[3] He recognizes that many will simply dismiss the query by answering, "Well of course this is my life! If it is not mine, whose else can it be?" A more thoughtful response would be to sit and feel its weight, as Palmer reflects:

> They remind me of moments when it is clear—if I have eyes to see—that the life I am living is not the same as the life that wants to live in me. In those moments I sometimes catch a glimpse of my true life, a life hidden like the river beneath the ice. And in the spirit of the poet, I wonder: What am I meant to do? Who am I meant to be?[4]

To further understand the false self and comprehend its pernicious ways, Paul delivers a fourfold description of the masked life. His first observation is that those who are conditioned by the false self are "spiritually unaware" and demonstrate this approach to life by "liv[ing] in the futility of their minds" (4:17) and being "darkened in their understanding" (4:18). Such descriptions imply an overcommitment to immediate experience and a lack of responsiveness to the mysterious workings of the Holy Spirit. For Paul, this happens for two reasons, of which the first is ignorance (3:18). When people are uneducated in the matters of the heart, they simply do not know better. They live, as Keating describes, in the "mythic membership consciousness," controlled by a commitment to race, clan, culture, and self.[5] "When we derive our identity from the social unit of which we are a member, we give the group unquestioning loyalty," he explains. "The sense of belonging to something important gives us feelings of security, pleasure and power."[6] As a result, we do not develop a sensitivity to legitimate needs expressed beyond our own circles.

A second reason is even more telling. Paul identifies it squarely as "hardness of heart" (3:18), specifically naming those at fault as "Gentiles" who consistently reject the drawings of the Holy Spirit, even as Pharaoh hardened his heart by rejecting the words of God through Moses, in spite of the accompanying miracles (Exod 7:13–14; 8:19). In a similar way, the writer of Hebrews cautions us to not build spiritual barriers by rejecting

---

3. Palmer, *Let Your Life Speak*, 1.
4. Palmer, *Let Your Life Speak*, 2.
5. Keating, *Invitation to Love*, 157–62.
6. Keating, *Invitation to Love*, 157.

the overtures of Abba and setting our minds on a path of resistance to God's revealed will.[7]

Second, Paul describes the false self as being desensitized and numbed out to the hurts that people carry. He captures this idea by stating that the Gentiles have "lost all sensitivity" and have given up any compassionate presence in favor of "licentiousness and greedy practices" (Eph 4:19). They are absent of any degree of empathy for the misfortunes of others, Paul suggests, as long as their own position is secure. Of course, it is impossible to respond to every need that arises—we do not have the emotional capacity to do so—but that is a different story than intentionally shutting down to protect oneself from the struggles of others. We mirror this perspective when we refuse to think about the contemporary refugee crisis and simply hunker down to enjoy our comfortable lives. It is possible that we choose this option because the need is great and as individuals we have limited means to act? However, as a faith community there are opportunities to express our solidarity as we pool our resources together and act compassionately as the people of God.

Third, the pseudo-persona is characterized as a self-centered entity. One expression of this worldview is a never-ending pursuit of gratification on an immediate level of sensation. The terms "licentiousness" and "greedy to practice every kind of impurity" (4:19) reveal a hunger for immediate sensorial highs. One's actions are based on a self-referential grid and result in passive indifference to the needs of others. It is obvious that such a mindset is bound to end in conflict as competing objectives clash, whether expressed on an individual level or in the sphere of geopolitics.

Fourth, the fictitious self describes an addicted self (4:19). They may be "hard addictions," like the inebriation of alcohol or the highs of drugs, creating obvious havoc; or more subtle "soft addictions," such as unbridled consumerism or obsessive cravings for food, coffee, or chocolate. In either case, the physical response is characterized in a twofold pattern: one, there is a physical craving that continues to build until the desire is met; two, following a brief respite, the "cycle of desire" intensifies until once again satiated. Roberta Bondi describes the ongoing impact of this phenomenon and one that we all face at some point:

> Hardly anyone who has ever said "if only I could have a ————, I would be happy" has found it to be so. A life that takes it meaning from eating, or sex, or owning things can never be fulfilled because

---

7. See Heb 3:7–8, 13, 15; 4:7.

the desires can never be permanently satisfied. These desires are alternately filled and recurring over and over. This phenomenon has been called "the cycle of desire."[8]

Thomas Merton refers to the false self as "the cult of the shadow" whereby one creates "an illusory self."[9] This fallacious self is a projection of who we want to be and of how we want to be seen. In its most destructive forms this pseudo-self is acted out through violence on our streets or with nations going to war. In both cases it is manifested through a "power-over" model whereby one party forcibly takes advantage over another without regard for tangential outcomes. This manufactured persona is also manifested in the boardrooms of the multinational corporations where fraud, greed, and power are pursued under the guise of corporate profit at the expense of the human and environmental impact. Isms of all sorts—racism, materialism, sexism, authoritarianism, totalitarianism, and hedonism—all share a commitment to the illusory self which impedes a compassionate concern for individuals and their existential needs. On a personal level it rises up as we desire our own satisfaction at the expense of our neighbor's needs as illustrated by the priest and Levite who pass by the injured man in the parable of the Good Samaritan (Luke 10:29–37). The way of the false self is directly opposed to the way of love as its primary concern is a projection of its own illusions of grandeur. There is no authentic regard for the "other" as it cannot imagine a world which transcends the importance of its own image. Obviously, the aberration of this fictitious guise is not one we want to adopt. With Palmer we see "the river beneath the ice" and it is this flowing water that our hearts long for rather than settling for the frozen tundra of the phantom self.

The Journey to the True Self

Alternatively, Paul encourages us to pursue the true self by employing a variety of phrases which speak to this animated lifestyle: "be renewed in the spirit of your minds" (Eph 4:23), "clothe yourself with the new self" (4:24), "[be] created according to the likeness of God" (4:24), "[be] created . . . in true righteousness and holiness" (4:24).[10] This authentic self

---

8. Bondi, *To Love as God Loves*, 60; see also May, *Addiction and Grace*, 58–60; and Davey, *Climbing the Spiritual Mountain*, 43–53.

9. Merton, *New Seeds of Contemplation*, 34.

10. See also Col 3:9–10 on the contrast of the true and false self.

is shaped by four characteristics which counter the negative properties of the manufactured persona. First, the genuine self is identified as being spiritually aware, which counters the spiritual unawareness of the pseudo persona. It is realized through a thinking pattern which is nurtured by spiritual truth and is demonstrated in Paul's phrase, "be[ing] renewed in the spirit of your minds" (4:23). Rahner captures this invigorating aspect of renewal when he makes the declaration, "If the heart is alive it thinks of God."[11] When we make this our practice we realize that the universe pulses with God's presence and we desire to tune in to his vibrations that resonate throughout creation. As a group of acoustic instruments spontaneously vibrate with one another as a single note is struck (known as sympathetic vibration), so the awakened heart resonates with Abba's overtures. The darkened understanding of the bogus self is replaced with the new mind of Christ, which liberates one from the domination of habitual self-centered behaviors and practices.

Second, the authentic person, giving up the insensitivity of the pseudo self, is shaped by compassion and sensitivity to others. Paul highlights this truth as he describes the renewed person in Christ becoming "more like the likeness of God in righteousness and holiness" (4:24). The old way of living based upon a myopic concern for one's personal advantage is replaced with a true regard for justice and compassionate living. It is instructive to note that the word "compassion" literally means "suffering with," which speaks to a solidarity of spirit in sharing the pain and woundedness of the other person. As the authors of *Compassion* suggest,

> This new self, the self of Jesus Christ, makes it possible for us to be compassionate as our Father is compassionate. Through union with him, we are lifted out of our competitiveness with each other into the divine wholeness. By sharing in the wholeness of the one in whom no competition exists, we can enter into new, compassionate relationships with each other.[12]

Rather than a dispirited rejection of another emanating from a numbed-out culture, this compassionate lifestyle is marked by a sensitivity to the needs of the other. It is shaped by a spirit of empathy expressed in a genuine regard for one's neighbor and for the purposes of God.

Third, the real self is characterized by love rather than the promotion of self. This is made evident in Paul's radical imperative, "Therefore,

---

11. Rahner, *Great Church Year*, 93.
12. McNeill et al., *Compassion*, 21.

be imitators of God, as beloved children, and live in love, as Christ loved us" (5:1–2). Here the apostle emphasizes the centrality of sacrificial love through a threefold repetition of the Greek root *agapaō*, "to love": first, we are identified as "God's beloved children"; second, we are called "to walk in love"; third, we have experienced ourselves this love, [even] "as Christ loved us." Mother Teresa points to the essential link between God's love and our own loving actions:

> There is only one love and this is the love of God. Once we love God deeply enough we will love our neighbor to the same extent because, as we grow in our love for God, we grow to respect all that He has created and to recognize and appreciate all the gifts He has given us. Then naturally we want to take care of all of them.[13]

We are encouraged to let go of the competitive self with its inveterate propensity for comparison and imitate the compassionate embodiment of Christ's love.

Fourth, the fully integrated individual is not characterized by addiction but with a caring, compassionate presence. The passions of anger, gluttony, avarice, impurity, acedia, and pride all emanate from the false self and share the characteristic of "the perversion of vision and the destruction of love."[14] In contrast, the true self, not driven by its own compulsions, transcends its own needs by seeking the well-being of others and embodying a largess of spirit which communicates the grace and mercy of Abba. A magnanimous sensibility is rooted in the central characteristics of bearing with others and long-suffering and is evidenced as we live out our everyday lives in patience. It is not a passive waiting, but a disciplined commitment which shares in the sufferings of others and perseveres with them through the difficulties of life. It is this patience which is at the center of compassion, as Paul writes in his sister Epistle to the Colossians: "As God's chosen ones, holy and beloved, clothe yourselves with compassion, kindness, humility, meekness, and patience" (Col 3:12).

It is important to recognize that putting on the new self is not like pulling up one's socks! It is not a matter of simply trying harder and doing a better job of living the virtuous life. Rather, the true self emerges as we open ourselves up to God and encounter his presence within us and his world (John 3:3). Indeed, it is about being discovered by God and experiencing

---

13. Mother Teresa, *Simple Path*, 80.
14. Bondi, *To Love as God Loves*, 58.

his renewing grace that leads to living a renovated life. Merton addresses this mysterious encounter in his work *New Seeds of Contemplation*:

> Ultimately the only way that I can be myself is to become identified with Him in Whom is hidden the reason and fulfillment of my existence. Therefore there is only one problem on which all my existence, my peace and happiness depend: to discover myself in discovering God. If I find Him I will find myself and if I find my true self I will find Him. [15]

Of course, this is not a simple task or an experience that happens all at once. It is why Paul advocates the need "to clothe yourselves with the new self" (Eph 4:24). It is a continuing work of renovation, or as coined in theological nomenclature, "a process of sanctification." If you like, we are to become pieces of living art where the Divine Sculptor shapes us in real time into the masterpieces he envisions. Consequently, it is imperative to keep aligning ourselves with God's will and to resist the draw of our own addictions. Even as old clothes are comfortable and we are slow to change them for new ones, so the old self is attractive because we know it so well. There is the temptation to resist the transformative path and settle for the meager comforts that the old person offers and miss out on the renewed self which leads to "the way everlasting" (Ps 139:24). Yet, by grace the Spirit draws us deeper into Christ and continues the spiritual overhaul of discarding our human pretensions for embracing the fully integrated life. As Paul affirms, we "are being transformed into the same image from one degree of glory to another; for this comes from the Lord, the Spirit" (2 Cor 3:18).

Revealing Our True Identity

Paul goes on to identify four practical ways the true self is expressed amidst the routines of everyday living. The first area of newness pertains to how the believer navigates the reality of anger within the community of faith. The apostle acknowledges that brokenness continues to be a part of church life causing significant turmoil and strife. As a result, divisiveness is to be dealt with promptly so that bitterness is not able to fester. "Be angry but do not sin," Paul writes. "Do not let the sun go down on your anger, and do not make room for the devil" (Eph 4:26–27; 31). The apostle understands that anger is an explosive passion and for the sake of the community it must be

---

15. Merton, *New Seeds of Contemplation*, 35–36.

curtailed in its impact and duration. Bondi offers an additional observation that "anger is more potentially destructive of love than any other passion. Furthermore, there is more danger of self-deception, as we tell ourselves we are correcting others for their own good."[16] Since conflict in the community often leads to dissension, we are advised to not make it our obsession, in spite of the popular notion that it is healthy to prolong and express our emotions as a way of releasing bottled up rage![17] Contrarily, Paul knows that anger quickly becomes an attachment which fuels the wrappings of the false self and impedes the emergence of the true self in Christ.

A second dimension of the new self speaks to the manner of discourse within the community of faith. Paul encourages believers to put away falsehood and to speak truthfully (4:25) as words of deception and falsehood have no place within the new humanity of Christ. Rather, our words are meant "to build each other up" and be instrumental in offering "grace to those who hear" (4:29). Paul goes beyond the simple imperative to stop hurting each other with judgmental words; he encourages the church to replace negative conversation with restorative patterns of speech. Any discussion which wounds the other person or disparages his or her character grieves the person of the Holy Spirit (4:30) and creates fractures within the body of Christ. Comprehending this truth, Bonhoeffer encourages the ministry of "holding one's tongue," affirming that "[h]e who holds his tongue in check controls both mind and body (Jas 3:2). Thus, it must be a decisive rule of every Christian fellowship that each individual is prohibited from saying much that occurs to him."[18] Throughout the years of our pastoral ministry we have seen many relationships go awry due to careless and undisciplined conversation needlessly erecting walls of separation. As Edward Farrell reminds us that "one vision is replaced by a greater vision,"[19] we see this worked out as Paul envisions a new self and a new humanity surpassing old patterns of self-centered living and hurtful speech.

A third demonstration of the new person in Christ is revealed through the practices of kindness and forgiveness (Eph 4:32). Kindness is seen in the Old Testament as a word which describes Yahweh's lovingkindness, compassion, and patience for his chosen people.[20] In the New Testa-

---

16. Bondi, *To Love as God Loves*, 74.
17. Bondi, *To Love as God Loves*, 74.
18. Bonhoeffer, *Life Together*, 91–92.
19. Farrell, *Beams of Prayer*, 130.
20. See Ps 18:50; 86:5; Isa 54:8; Jer 9:24; Hos 11:4.

ment kindness points to the life of Jesus and the qualities he embodies of patience, tenderheartedness, gentleness, meekness, and humility (Matt 5:1–12). John Stott notes that the Greek word *chrēstos*, or "kind," demonstrates an obvious assonance with the name of Christ: "Christians from the beginning saw its peculiar appropriateness" as a Christlike quality.[21] Forgiveness plays a prominent role in Jesus' teaching as he encourages his disciples to ask for forgiveness and to forgive others in their prayers: "And forgive us our debts, as we also have forgiven our debtors"; "For if you forgive others their trespasses, your Heavenly Father will also forgive you" (Matt 6:12, 14). As kindness and forgiveness radiate from God (Eph 2:7), so these qualities are to be markers of his beloved children, who seek to imitate their Heavenly Father (Eph 5:1–2).

I am reminded of a childhood reminiscence from Steve Bell, Canadian singer-songwriter, who tells the story of Jean Vanier, the founder of L'Arche, visiting his family home during a time his father was chaplain at Stony Mountain Penitentiary. During the occasion he remembers going outside to play with his sisters while Vanier intently watched from the porch. Steve was so struck by the kindness in the visitor's eyes that he turned around to see who he was looking at, only to discover that Vanier was looking at him! As an adult, he writes that this moment of "being seen—really *seen*—and delighted in" has stayed with him over the years, and indeed, has become a touchstone for his own standing as a beloved child of God.[22] It seems to me that the contemporary church is not generally known for its gentle and kindly ways but is often experienced as a place of judgmentalism. Many feel critiqued when entering a church rather than receiving a kind smile or genuine welcome that might set them at ease. None of this fits Paul, who invites us to see individuals as persons created in God's image and who deserve to be seen even as Steve felt accepted and esteemed by Jean Vanier years ago. Demonstrating kindness is a crucial aspect of the authentic self, reaching beyond tolerance for those who live differently, and becomes an active engagement expressing generosity and goodwill.

A fourth expression of living authentically is to embrace a life of love even "as Christ loved us" (Eph 5:2). It is interesting to note that the Greek culture of the day sought to identify a core virtue which bound the remaining attributes together.[23] For Paul, the harmonizing quality is found in love, as

---

21. Stott, *God's New Society*, 190.
22. Huff, *Bent Hope*, 176.
23. Donelson, *Colossians, Ephesians*, 47.

he proffers, "Above all, clothe yourselves with love, which binds everything in perfect harmony" (Col 3:14). Through this image Paul invites us to move beyond our private world and embrace the greater good, which is most effectively accomplished through a life of love. There is no way to realize this other than engaging our everyday world for Abba, or as Karl Rahner muses, "If there is any path at all . . . it must lead through the very middle of [our] ordinary [lives]."[24] All of our God thoughts must come down to an everyday expression of love; if not, our religious words and ideas are, as Paul opines, "puffed up hot air" (1 Cor 13:4). It is as simple and as hard as that, for as we live out our lives in love we demonstrate the presence of the Divine Family. As we do so together, we become the passionate bride of Christ, discarding the wrappings of the false self for the apparel of the new, enabling us to carry out our calling in authenticity and efficacy.

We began the chapter with Thomas Merton. We end with him again, as we pray with him:

> Give me the strength that waits upon You in silence and peace. Give me humility in which alone is rest, and deliver me from pride which is the heaviest of burdens. And possess my whole heart and soul with the simplicity of love. Occupy my whole life with the one thought and the one desire of love, that I may love not for the sake of merit, not for the sake of perfection, not for the sake of virtue, not for the sake of sanctity, but for You alone. For there is only one thing that can satisfy love and reward it, and that is You alone.[25]

Questions for Reflection

1. Paul characterizes the false self in four ways: (1) it is spiritually unaware; (2) it is insensitive to the needs of others; (3) it is self-centered; (4) it is defined by addictive behavior. Which of these four aspects are most evident when you are under the influence of the false self? Spend some time writing in your journal how this process works itself out in the shape of your week.

2. The true self is revealed as we overcome the negativity of the false self; that is, we become spiritually aware—sensitive to the concerns of others, not controlled by selfish desires, revealing a compassionate

---

24. Rahner, *Encounters with Silence*, 48.
25. Merton, *New Seeds of Contemplation*, 45.

presence in our everyday life. As you reflect upon your journey write down some of the ways your true self is emerging where previously your false self dominated. Remember to not be discouraged when the bogus self rises up. Simply come before Abba with an honest and receptive heart and begin again.

3. The apostle Paul is quite practical when he discusses the areas of engagement that reveal our path to spiritual transformation. For example, how do we deal with anger? Do our speech patterns build others up or tear them down? Does kindness characterize us or a spirit of bitterness, or perhaps an unwillingness to forgive? These are not simply esoteric ideas but concrete paths that provide opportunities for building bridges within our communities. During your prayer times this week ask the Holy Spirit to guide you into a deeper awareness of how you are either impeding or showing the true self as you live out your day.

9

A Transformative Journey

Ephesians 5:1–20

"What we choose to fight is so tiny!
What fights with us is so great!
If only we would let ourselves be dominated
as things do by some immense storm,
we would become strong too, and not need names.

When we win it's with small things,
and the triumph itself makes us small.
What is extraordinary and eternal
does not *want* to be bent by us ..."

Rainer Maria Rilke

"*Therefore, be imitators of God, as beloved children, and live in love,*
  as Christ loved us and gave himself up for us, a fragrant offering and sacrifice to God.

But fornication and impurity of any kind, or greed, must not even be mentioned among you,
  as is proper among saints.
Entirely out of place is obscene, silly, and vulgar talk;
  but instead, let there be thanksgiving.
Be sure of this, that no fornicator or impure person, or one who is greedy (that is, an idolater),

has any inheritance in the kingdom of Christ and of God.
Let no one deceive you with empty words,
> *for because of these things the wrath of God comes on those who are disobedient.*
>> *Therefore do not be associated with them.*

For once you were darkness, but now in the Lord you are light.
Live as children of light—for the fruit of the light is found in all that is good and right and true.
Try to find out what is pleasing to the Lord.

Take no part in the unfruitful works of darkness, but instead expose them.
> *For it is shameful even to mention what such people do secretly;*
> *but everything exposed by the light becomes visible,*
> *for everything that becomes visible is light.*
> *Therefore it says, 'Sleeper, awake! Rise from the dead, and Christ will shine on you.'*

Be careful then how you live, not as unwise people but as wise,
> *making the most of the time, because the days are evil.*
> *So do not be foolish, but understand what the will of the Lord is.*

Do not get drunk with wine, for that is debauchery;
> *but be filled with the Spirit,*
>> *as you sing psalms and hymns and spiritual songs among yourselves,*
>>> *singing and making melody to the Lord in your hearts,*
>>> *giving thanks to God the Father at all times*
>>> *and for everything in the name of our Lord Jesus Christ."*
>>>> *(Ephesians 5:1–20)*

A couplet from Rainer Maria Rilke often plays itself out in the back of my mind: "All of you undisturbed cities, haven't you ever longed for the Enemy?"[1] The lines create a disquieting internal disturbance as they bump

---

1. Rilke, *Selected Poems*, 41.

up against a comfortable lifestyle seemingly sheltered from the world's unrest. It seems to me that I am not alone in erecting walls to impede the invading forces that threaten my security. Yet in the lurking shadows there are longings for upheaval and for engagement in the great battle which transcends the desire for an imperturbable existence. Rilke speaks perceptibly as he envisions the relentless labor of "the Enemy": "He is the one who breaks down the walls, and when he works, he works in silence."[2] This quiet observation suggests that God is not overly concerned with whether or not we live comfortable lives; rather, he is interested in our desire for casting off inauthenticity and replacing it with the authenticity of the new. To this end God is passionate about our success in completing the transformative journey, and works with precision to raze any barrier that we glibly construct in the pursuit of living conventional lives. As a result, it may be helpful to consider the following questions as we continue to reflect on our faith journey: How do we respond to the Great Invader who takes siege of our comfortable existence? Do we close ranks and resist at all costs the one who desires to travel with us? Or, do we open our hearts to his renovating power and accept the invitation to rest in his arms of love?

Living as Children of God

Returning to Paul's letter, we see that the apostle commences the new unit with a reminder that we are the beloved children of God (Eph 5:1) and that this relationship of intimacy is realized through Christ's sacrifice, made on our behalf, "as a fragrant offering to God" (5:2). Through the oblation of Jesus we are ushered into God's kingdom and share the elevated status of being named the daughters and sons of the Heavenly King. This action of salvific love is beautifully presented by C. S. Lewis in his children's novel *The Lion, the Witch and the Wardrobe*, as Aslan, the majestic lion, takes the place of Edmund, who has been condemned to die on the stone table by the wiles of the Wicked Witch.[3] In a similar manner, through an act of sacrificial love Christ dies for us on the cross so that we do not have to pay the penalty for our estrangement from God. This substitutionary act is funded by Christ's profound love, even as we observe the self-giving love of parents around the globe for the welfare of their precious children. As a result, we are invited

---

2. Rilke, *Selected Poems*, 41.
3. See Lewis, *Lion, the Witch and the Wardrobe*, 170.

to receive this amazing gift and to do so by "liv[ing] in love" (Eph 5:2), and casting it as the center of our lives and faith communities.

Paul highlights this truth by alluding to the Greco-Roman practice of basing a child's education upon the imitation of the master.[4] In the first century such emulation was standard as the student mimicked the mores and values of the tutor. Indeed, on various occasions Paul exemplifies this custom by exhorting his spiritual children to imitate his faith practice (1 Cor 11:1; Phil 3:17). What is exceptional in the Ephesians text is Paul's invitation to "be[come] imitators of God" (Eph 5:1). This is the only time in the New Testament where believers are called to directly imitate God himself. Through this overture Paul reminds the faith community that they are on a great adventure of not only becoming like Christ but of becoming like the Father. Our ultimate destiny is to share in the life of the Divine Family, whereby we live as God's beloved children and enthusiastically follow his Son Jesus Christ in our own spheres of influence as we engage in kingdom work.

To ensure that the call for the imitation of God does not simply become an abstract idea, Paul elaborates on the specifics of the invocation. The first area he addresses is the rampant immorality characteristic of the broader community. He notes that "fornication and impurity of any kind, or greed, must not even be mentioned among you" (Eph 5:3) and "no fornicator or impure person . . . has any inheritance in the kingdom of Christ and of God" (5:5). Paul highlights this concern knowing that a dominant institution in Ephesus is the Temple of Artemis with its practice of cultic prostitution.[5] He is also well aware that in the Greco-Roman world sexual promiscuity is commonly practiced and not considered an unacceptable behavior even within the marriage covenant. The apostle knows that *eros* has the ability to quickly become an attachment which acts as a spiritual block in the journey of faith. This understanding is illustrated as he links impurity and greed and asserts that both are expressions of "idolatry" (5:5). Paul identifies avarice (greed) to be a spiritual inhibitor (5:5) knowing that it has the ability to quickly turn into an all-consuming power. Roberta Bondi comments on the nature of avarice, saying, "[It] has to do with believing that possessions actually provide far more security than they do, a very common misconception in our materialistic culture."[6] Unrestrained desires for both material possessions and sensual pleasure are behaviors which produce heightened

---

4. See Talbert, *Ephesians and Colossians*, 123.
5. See Stott, *God's New Society*, 192; Donelson, *Colossians, Ephesians*, 97.
6. Bondi, *To Love as God Loves*, 72.

physical reactions. Due to the nature of these somatic responses, they rapidly progress into compulsive behaviors which Paul curtly names "idols." As a result, Paul cautions the Ephesians to be on guard against such practices and to not forsake the greater pursuit of knowing God for passing sensations that cannot satisfy or be fully satiated.

Alternatively, Paul exhorts the community to turn away from sexual licentiousness (5:3–5) and replace it with "thanksgiving" (5:4). By doing so he counsels the Ephesians not to settle for a life of lust but to pursue a life of love, not to be shaped by discontentment but to embrace gratitude, and not to be defined by despair but to be motivated by hope (5:5). In short, he wants the Ephesian community—and us—to receive the abundant life of living as children of God and to engage it each day by walking in the awareness of Abba's presence.

We catch a glimpse of this transformative work through the story C. S. Lewis tells in his fantasy *The Great Divorce*. He imagines a group of tourists who travel from hell to heaven to see if they might like to change their permanent residence. One of the tourists is an apparition who walks about with a lizard of lust sitting on his shoulder which is constantly chattering into his ear. As the ghost tours the new environs he is greeted by an angel who claims that he can dispose of the lizard if the ghost agrees to it. The traveler pauses and considers the proposal. On the one hand, he hates the constant muttering and lustful power it has over him; but on the other hand, the creature has been his long-term companion. Of course, the lizard is greatly upset with the angel's suggestion and urges his comrade to leave heaven immediately! The angel patiently encourages the visitor with the truth that his life will be far superior without the lustful beast but the choice must be his. "May I kill it?" In a moment of desperation, the ghost agrees and the angel delivers a mighty blow. The ghost falls to the ground crying out, as if dead. The story shows the ghost emerging into a "newly-made son of Adam," standing up free from his long-term accuser. However, to his great surprise, the lizard itself is transformed before his eyes into a silvery white, golden-maned stallion. Amazed, the renewed pilgrim mounts the powerful steed and they joyfully ride off into the deeper realms of heaven.[7] I wonder what graces God has reserved for us if we would give up our resistance and live authentically as his beloved children? Perhaps, we would also be amazed and see our compulsions transformed into God's beautiful gifts bringing abundance to ourselves and to others?

---

7. Lewis, *Great Divorce*, 82–88.

Living as Children of Light

Paul continues his encouragement to put on the true self by inviting his readers "to live as children of light." He does this by employing the bold language of "once you were darkness, but now in the Lord you are light" (Eph 5:8), indicating that they were not simply living in darkness but embodied darkness itself. By this Paul refers to the obscurity of the false self, which contains no measure of true life but simply comprises the machinations of ego-centered desires: How do I impress others? How am I perceived? Do people know who I am? How much power and control do I have? These questions suggest a speculative quality and desire to promote oneself at the expense of others rather than enlivening one's substantive inner person actually seen by God. Rather than playing the competitive game of winning or losing in the collection of external accolades, Paul enjoins the Ephesians to manifest true light by engaging in "all that is good and right and true" (5:9).

Another angle on Paul's exhortation is not to engage in comparison, which, again, is inherently ego driven; rather, to stay centered in the light by expressing goodness and kindness in what we say and do. The apostle encourages us to move in this direction by employing the common-sense suggestion, "Try to find out what is pleasing to the Lord" (5:10). Here we seek the Holy Spirit's orientation in every situation we encounter. We know that the Scriptures give us a direction for living but do not provide specific directions; hence, there is a need for qualitative listening for intuiting the Spirit's leading into the way of fecundity.

Walking in the light means giving up our attachments to the darkness. Paul does not say that the works of darkness are unpleasing, but that they are "unfruitful" (5:11). Certain actions the false self engenders are no doubt pleasant as experienced in the gratification of the senses or the highs from addictive behaviors.[8] What Paul understands, however, is that they are fundamentally unhelpful and do not lead us into spiritual abundance. Walking in darkness does not enable us to fulfill our true destiny or to capture the essence of our deepest longings. It is only by walking in the light that the true self emerges and grows into the integrated authentic self that Abba desires us to know. To make this point Paul employs a baptismal refrain, "Sleeper, awake! Rise from the dead, and Christ will shine on you"

---

8. See Ps 141:4; Prov 23:3, 6.

(5:14).[9] It is as we move into the light that our paths become clear, for as Paul notes, "everything that becomes visible is light" (5:14). Furthermore, as we pursue the lighted path the attraction of the darkness wanes and its influence in our lives diminishes.

A powerful example of transformation is presented in the 1996 film *Moll Flanders* (inspired by the novel *Moll Flanders* by Daniel Defoe), depicting the life of a destitute street woman in eighteenth-century London. Moll's life consists of a continuing series of degradations due to poverty, prostitution, abuse, and violence all flowing from her life as an orphaned child. She demonstrates an understandable mistrust of men and relies on her own wiles for eking out her survival, doing so primarily through thievery and by embracing a bordello life. Moll's renewal takes place ironically through her connections with two different men: the tender care offered by Hibble (the servant of the bordello's Madam) and a loving liaison that unfolds with Jonathan, an unconventional and charismatic artist. As a result of these healing relationships she abandons her wayfaring lifestyle and matures into an integrated individual who experiences a metamorphosis as a confident and joyful Moll Flanders. As we consider the fictional Moll's transformation, we cast our eyes in the direction of exchanging lives of walking in darkness for embracing the even greater light of the Divine Family.

It is apparent that walking in the light is an intentional path requiring daily choices which move us away from darkness and towards the love of God. This journey from the ego-centered self towards the authentic person is a conscious battle of resisting the allure of an epicurean lifestyle and choosing to walk in the path of beneficence. On a daily basis the Ephesians faced the celebrated attractions of the Artemis Temple, which were a mainstay of the city's cultural life. We have a window into their communal patterns as we read of the riot that took place in Ephesus when the artisan trade of making silver shrines to Artemis was threatened due to the expansion of Christianity (Acts 19:23–41). As Luke records, a great crowd filled the 25,000-person stadium and chanted in unison for two hours, "Great is Artemis of the Ephesians," elevating religious pride in the goddess and effectively cutting short Paul's ministry in the region. On account of the riot, Christians living in the city experienced constant pressure to resume their homage to the goddess and to participate in the ceremonies designed in her honor. Over and over the faith community felt the attraction of the fertility cult and were faced with the decision of forsaking or staying true to their

---

9. Martin, *Ephesians, Colossians*, 63.

Christian calling. In our day it is no different. Our culture is fascinated with darkness and the entertainment industry is jam-packed with films, television shows, and gaming that concentrate on themes related to demons, the devil, violence, war, and the satiation of the senses. The challenge we face in overcoming this onslaught is to consistently center our lives in Jesus so that darkness is replaced with the light of God, who desires that we know his abounding love in the reality of our everyday (Jas 4:5–8).

Living as Children of Wisdom

The final strand in Paul's exhortation is an invitation to live "not as unwise people but as wise" (Eph 5:15), paralleling the wisdom literature of the time. Furthermore, we note that throughout Paul's letters there is a call to live in wisdom. See Romans 12:2; Philippians 1:9–11; Colossians 1:9–10; and Colossians 4:5–6 for his concern as he follows both the Jewish and Greek traditions. The Jewish community had a longstanding wisdom tradition exemplified in the books of Proverbs, Psalms, Ecclesiastes, and Job—all providing guidance for adhering to God's purposes. The Greeks also valued sapiential literature and respected the call to live a virtuous life as seen in the works of Seneca, Plutarch, Plato, and Socrates.[10] The receptiveness of these two communities for wisdom teaching provides Paul with a ready audience for unpacking his understanding of "liv[ing] not as unwise but as wise" and "be[ing] careful then how you live" (Eph 5:15). For Paul, the appeal is not about pursuing intellectual knowledge but living a life committed to the fear of God. It is not about raising ones IQ but about making daily choices which honor the Divine Family.

The first component that Paul addresses is the subject of time, as he encourages the Ephesians to value and make the most of the time which they have at their disposal (5:16). The Greek word the apostle uses for time is *kairos*, making the most of the time, and not the more common word *chronos*. Simpson and Bruce observe that "the common rendering is inadequate; *kairos* implies a critical epoch, a special opportunity which may soon pass; 'grasp it,' says the apostle; 'buy it up while it lasts.'"[11] Paul's entreaty is to engage the doors that are opening and to not let the possibilities slip away through lack of effort or enthusiasm. Scott Peck, in his work *A World*

---

10. See Talbert, *Ephesians and Colossians*, 130–35.
11. Simpson and Bruce, *Ephesians/Colossians*, 299.

Waiting to Be Born, highlights time's preciousness, arguing that an intentional embracing and use of it is a quality essential for effective living.[12]

Too often we waste our time and miss out on opportunities because of a combination of apathy and boredom. To this point Paul employs a term from economics, *exagorazō*, which translates as "making the most of," "redeem," or "deliver" (5:16), appealing to the individual to take advantage of a good deal or buy something up while the opportunity exists.[13] I think of the city of Cochabamba, with its great market "The Cancha," where one can enter into a labyrinth of narrow pathways lined with diminutive stalls and find items of every description at bargain prices! On various occasions I have taken Paul's advice and entered the maze to buy up good deals of jewelry, leather goods, or artisan products to give as gifts when returning from my travels in Bolivia.

Alongside the injunction on time is Paul's exhortation concerning discernment: "So do not be foolish, but understand what the will of the Lord is" (5:17). The invitation is for wise action founded on prayer and self-reflection rather than decisions based upon manipulation or coercion. It takes a thoughtful and meditative spirit to discern the *kairos* moment so that wise and fruitful actions are the results. In one of Jesus' parables some anxious servants come to their master saying that the planted field is full of darnel. Worried, they ask him if they should enter the field and pull out the darnel. The master's wise response is that it is not yet the opportune time for it would result in damage to the planted crop. It is better to wait until the day of harvest for on that day the darnel can be safely removed while the wheat is being harvested (Matt 13:24–30). So it is with us. There is a need for action but it is best served when it is well prepared and timely.

Paul follows his positive call for wisdom with a negative one—"to not engage in debauchery"—and provides an example of such dereliction in "getting drunk with wine" (Eph 5:18). Debauchery counts as one of the "medieval passions" along with gluttony, avarice, impurity, sadness, and anger, which are all enervating characteristics of the false self. Such an understanding recognizes that profligacy is not limited to alcohol, drugs, food, or promiscuous conduct but speaks to one's addictions or behaviors that consume and prevent one from living the virtuous life. It raises questions concerning the nature of our true god and the unnamed idols in our lives. Queries like these reveal the sticky quality of the false self and how

---

12. Peck, *World Waiting to Be Born*, 81–85.
13. Kubo, *Reader's Greek-English Lexicon*, 186.

it seeks to wrap itself in greed, power, materialism, and lust to give itself a substantial form of existence.

In order to resist such passions Paul encourages us to "be filled with the Spirit" (5:18), which can be understood as the Spirit's ongoing filling—present tense—taking place through the conduit of an open heart. Receptivity of this nature is funded by the response of heartfelt worship described by Paul as "sing[ing] psalms and hymns and spiritual songs among yourselves, singing and making melody to the Lord in your hearts" (5:19). Worship of this type fills our hearts and minds with light rather than darkness. It engages both mind and spirit in the wonder and beauty of our Holy God through an experience which is both creative and vital. Such a spirit of adoration lifts us above the angst and apathy of the present age and renews us by the energizing Spirit, who incarnates the creative power of Abba in our lives.

Finally, Paul encourages his readers to pursue a life of gratitude. In his long, complex directive, the apostle ends the sentence with the clause, "giving thanks to God the Father at all times and for everything in the name of our Lord Jesus Christ" (5:20), signaling its importance. A spirit of thanks is a recurring refrain in the writings of Paul as we observe elsewhere: "Do not worry about anything, but in everything by prayer and supplication with thanksgiving let your requests be made known to God" (Phil 4:6); "Be prepared to endure everything with patience, while joyfully giving thanks to the Father, who has enabled you to share in the inheritance of the saints in the light" (Col 1:11–12); "Give thanks in all circumstances; for this is the will of God in Christ Jesus for you" (1 Thess 5:18).[14]

St. Paul's encouragement to embrace a spirit of gratitude is not an eyes-shut outlook pertaining to human suffering, but a fundamental conviction that God ultimately "makes all things well," as Julian of Norwich famously declared.[15] Gratitude is a belief and practice which undoes the negative impact that complaining has on the human spirit. Gratitude can still come from one who understands that life is not always fair. As Rahner muses, this is "our one chance to be [a] Christian," so let us engage our lives with buoyant and grateful hearts.[16] I appreciate the encouraging words from Georgia O'Keeffe, who knew much resistance as a female painter in a misogynistic artistic culture, as she advised, "Whether

---

14. See also 1 Tim 2:1–2; Col 3:15–17; Rom 15:8–13.

15. Julian of Norwich, *Revelations of Divine Love*, 130–32.

16. Rahner, *Great Church Year*, 298.

you succeed or not is irrelevant, there is no such thing. Making your unknown known is the important thing . . . and keeping the unknown always beyond."[17] Such a spirit of stick-to-itiveness flows well from the discipline of gratitude and is a keen support for the person who desires to walk in the ways of wisdom and fruitfulness.

Embracing Transformation

We are God's workmanship and he is molding us into living art that transcends any rendition of the false self for the realization of a glorious, authentic self destined for eternal life (Eph 2:10). It is a process characterized by an increasing awareness of belonging to Abba, a growing determination to walk in his light, and an intensifying desire to walk in wisdom as his children. During this transformational journey we continue to open our hearts and minds to Jesus who by his Spirit renews our minds (Eph 4:23). Paul goes on to admonish the Ephesian Christians to "cloth[e] yourselves with the new self, which is being renewed in knowledge according to the image of its creator" (Col 3:10). A Spanish translation interpreting *renovar* or *renovando* provides a helpful insight as it renders the phrase "to be renewed in the spirit of your minds" (Eph 4:23) as "being renovated until reaching perfect knowledge," which conjures up the image of an edifice undergoing renovation through a systematic revitalization project.[18] Abba is, indeed, renovating our entire persons so that one day we will match the image of his glorious Son Jesus Christ! C. S. Lewis, in his inimitable way and borrowing the parable from his mentor George MacDonald, provides an unforgettable picture of this renovation:

> Imagine yourself as a living house. God comes in to rebuild that house. At first, perhaps, you can understand what He is doing. He is getting the drains right and stopping the leaks in the roof and so on: you knew that those jobs needed doing and so you are not surprised. But presently he starts knocking the house about in a way that hurts abominably and does not seem to make sense. What on earth is He up to? The explanation is that He is building quite a different house from the one you thought of—throwing out a new wing here, putting on an extra floor there, running up towers, making courtyards. You thought you were going to be made into

---

17. O'Keeffe, exhibition at the Art Gallery of Ontario, Summer 2017.
18. Biblia de Jerusalén Latino Americana.

a decent little cottage: but He is building a palace. He intends to come and live in it Himself.[19]

Our ultimate transfiguration is so breathtaking, it behooves us to take our spiritual pilgrimage seriously and to cooperate intentionally with the Spirit's work of reconstruction. Throughout our day—in every moment—we are invited to be receptive to the Spirit's guidance through a process of inward listening and to avoid lapsing into patterns of the false self. As Paul indicates in the preceding section of his letter, the journey towards authenticity is best shown in our interpersonal dynamics: How do we deal with anger? (Eph 4:26–27). Do our speech patterns help or hurt others? (4:29). What role does kindness play in our daily routines? (4:32) Are we ready to forgive others or do we hold on to a spirit of bitterness? (4:32). When we find ourselves imitating Jesus to a greater degree we can have confidence that the renovation process is underway and we are moving in the direction of Abba's foundational love.

As we close this unit, we are reminded of Teilhard's observation concerning three types of people that inhabit our planet: first, the Tired—those who are daunted by the challenges of life and are simply worn out from the daily grind; second, the Hedonists—those who covet beyond everything else pleasure, comfort, and sensorial delights; third, the Enthusiasts—those who seek integration of mind, spirit, and body by maximizing each day as an opportunity for authentic living.[20] From Teilhard's perspective, the future of the Planet's well-being rests in the hands of the Enthusiasts, who seek an integrated and joyful relationship with God and his creation. To this end he encourages us to join their ranks for it is in this direction that we experience God's abundance and become his instruments for global peace. We return to the epigraph with which this chapter began—the poet Rilke's challenge. We face the "eternal Enemy"—this one who seeks our utter transformation through engagement in the Great Battle. We do not want to settle for "small" or "tiny" skirmishes. The Invader steers us in this direction by tearing down the walls that we scurry to erect in our desperation for security, comfort, and certainty! Using the poet's language, Abba dons the role of the "antagonist" because he delights in our absolute metamorphosis, resulting in a perfect inheritance for those who bear the name of God (Rev 3:12). As the passionate bride of Christ, we are called

---

19. Lewis, *Mere Christianity*, 205.
20. Teilhard de Chardin, *Toward the Future*, 110–12.

to zealously embrace this great work of renewal so that God's reign might come to fruition on planet Earth.

Questions for Reflection

1. Rilke portrays a scene in which we build walls to protect our comfortable lives but in doing so limit our capacity for spiritual growth. As you consider your faith walk, identify the walls that you are constructing which are actually counterproductive in the journey towards the true self.

2. During the Greco-Roman era imitation was a foundational element of the educational process. Paul elevates this accepted norm by inviting us to become "imitators of God" even as Jesus practiced through his life of sacrificial love. Write in your journal the ways that you are succeeding in this noble enterprise. Write where you are missing the mark. During the coming week pray over both sides of the equation and listen for Abba's voice as he guides you forward.

3. Walking in the light requires us to be intentional in the making of positive choices. As you consider your choices, can you identify areas that you would like to reshape? In the coming week try to implement these changes and evaluate the impact on your experience of walking with Jesus.

4. Paul encourages us "to make the most of our time," which addresses the two fields of *chronos*, or chronological time, and *kairos*, or time of opportunity. Reflect on the use of your time from both perspectives and evaluate whether you are using your time wisely. For example, try tracking your time this week and note how many hours you spend on "screen time." Any surprises? In terms of *kairos*, is there an opportunity looming which invites further reflection and engagement?

10

The Bride of Christ

Ephesians 5:21–33

"'You are beautiful, but you are empty,' he went on. 'One could not die for you. To be sure, an ordinary passerby would think that my rose looked just like you—the rose that belongs to me. But in herself alone she is more important than all the hundreds of you other roses: because it is she that I have watered; because it is she that I have put under the glass globe; because it is she that I have sheltered behind the screen; because it is for her that I have killed the caterpillars (except the two or three that we saved to become butterflies); because it is she that I have listened to, when she grumbled, or boasted, or even sometimes when she said nothing. Because she is *my* rose.'"

Antoine de Saint-Exupéry, The Little Prince

"Be subject to one another out of reverence for Christ.

Wives, be subject to your husband as you are to the Lord.
    For the husband is the head of the wife just as Christ is the head of the church,
        the body of which he is the Savior.
    Just as the church is subject to Christ,
        so also wives ought to be, in everything, to their husbands.

Husbands, love your wives,
> *just as Christ loved the church and gave himself up for her,*
> *in order to make her holy by cleansing her with the washing of water by the word,*
> *so as to present the church to himself in splendour,*
>> *without a spot or wrinkle or anything of the kind—yes,*
>> *so that she may be holy and without blemish.*

In the same way, husbands should love their wives as they do their own bodies.
He who loves his wife loves himself.
> *For no one ever hates his own body, but he nourishes and tenderly cares for it,*
> *just as Christ does for the church,*
>> *because we are members of his body.*

For this reason a man will leave his father and mother and be joined to his wife,
> *and the two will become one flesh.*

This is a great mystery, and I am applying it to Christ and the church.
Each of you, however, should love his wife as himself, and a wife should respect her husband." (Ephesians 5:21–33)

The small Dutch island of Saba amidst a handful of isles known as the Leeward Islands is located at the juncture of the northeastern Caribbean Sea and the western Atlantic Ocean. It is essentially a potentially active volcano rising up from the clear turquoise waters and is famous in the diving community for its underwater pinnacles. From Toronto my dive partner and I travel to St. Maarten and then catch a De Havilland Twin Otter aircraft to reach Saba. The prosaic twelve-minute flight escalates into an energy rush as the rocky outcrop welcomes us with its volcanic cliffs and the shortest commercial runway in the world—the length of an aircraft carrier—blasted out of the volcano's slope during the 1960s! A unique feature of the island is the only true cloud forest in the Caribbean, characterized by non-stop showers at the highest altitudes. Towards the end of our dive trip we hike up the volcanic peaks to enjoy the foliage, including mahogany trees, luscious palms, and an assortment of berry brambles and birdlife. In spite of the forest's mystical beauty, including a mighty deluge, what is most impressive is the symbiosis between the cloud and the volcanic crag, reminding me of Antoine de Saint-Exupéry's description of the Little Prince's love for his beloved rose.

Paul presents a similar portrayal of Christ and his loving relationship with the church as he continues his Letter to the Ephesians. It is important to note that the apostle does not always present his message through a linear argument, or as one commentator writes, "He does not always write in strictly logical sequences in which each statement follows obviously from the preceding one. Rather, he often presents a cluster of statements that, taken together, paint a picture."[1] This is the case in the present passage, where Paul repeats the word *ecclesia*, or "church," on six occasions, and also the name of "Christ" or "Savior" a corresponding six times. The result is an artistic rendering which weaves Christ and his church together in an inseparable and loving union. As van Breemen exclaims,

> The love of God through Christ is indeed bottomless. It can never be exhausted or fully known. His love is a constant self-giving, even as the sun constantly nurtures our planet. No matter how deeply we are immersed in God's love, we never reach the bottom, since that does not exist. God's love has no limit, no end.[2]

It is in this manner that Christ loves his church and holds on to it with an ardent embrace even as he desires a commensurate response from his people.

Christ's Passion for His Church

As Paul continues his discourse he turns to the import of the household code, or *Haustafel*, a commonplace template of household management found in the Hellenistic Jewish codes, according to Philo and Josephus; the Greco-Roman world, emphasized in the writings of Seneca, Plato, and Aristotle; and in early Christian literature as found in Polycarp, Clement,

---

1. E. Palmer, *Integrity*, 159.
2. Breemen, *God Who Won't Let Go*, 28.

and Chrysostom.[3] In this code Paul, sounding very similar to his Greco-Roman and Hellenistic Jewish counterparts, addresses the relationships between members of the household, including husbands, wives, children, and slaves, as he enumerates the responsibilities between the different members.[4] Astonishingly new in the first century is the apostle's call for mutual submission, or *hypotassomai*, as found in the opening line of the unit, "Be subject to one another out of reverence for Christ" (Eph 5:21). All of the relationships within the household management are to be marked by mutual submission and love where each person is respected and valued, including the household slaves (Eph 6:9; 1 Cor 7:4).[5] The thread of agape love between members of the same household is a breakthrough in a society marked by extreme class distinctions and a variation of roles. Paul does not abrogate the household code, but fills it with the center of agape love as modeled by Christ's selfless love for his church. Hence, wives are to submit to (love) their husbands even as the church is to submit to Christ (Eph 5:23), and husbands are to love their wives even as Christ loves his church (5:25). Mutual love is the key for understanding Paul's presentation of the household dynamic, which is differentiated from the cultural practice based on position and power.

The significance of this theme is highlighted as Paul segues back and forth between Christ's love for his church and his understanding of how household relationships are to be shaped by the power of love. As one looks closely at the text, a dominant metaphor that emerges is Christ's love for his bride, the church. To this end, Paul employs a variety of phrases which paint a portrait of Christ's profound love for the new humanity of God. The first brushstroke presents Christ as the head of the church even as the husband is the head of the wife (5:23). The identification of Christ as "head" is often interpreted in terms of hierarchy but the alternative reading of "head" as "source" is compelling. In this context, Scanzoni and Hardesty make the instructive observation that "the 'head' of this living, growing organism is not its ruler but the source of its life. *Kephalē* is used most synonymously with *archē*, or 'beginning,' somewhat similar to our use of the 'headwaters of a river' or 'fountainhead.'"[6] Within this interpretation Christ is seen as the source of the church in that its very life flows from his life; without him

---

3. See Talbert, *Ephesians and Colossians*, 136–39.
4. Talbert, *Ephesians and Colossians*, 136–39.
5. See Evans, *Woman in the Bible*, 74; and Muddiman, *Epistle to the Ephesians*, 257.
6. Scanzoni and Hardesty, *All We're Meant to Be*, 30–31.

the church does not exist. In a similar manner, God creates Eve from Adam as depicted in the creation story (Gen 2:21).

A second image proclaims Christ to be "the Savior of his church" (Eph 5:23). Indeed, the church is seen as the body of Christ which comes into existence through his salvific work. This designation for Christ as Savior is an essential characteristic in Paul's nomenclature as it challenges the popular understanding of savior status granted to many of the Greco-Roman gods and particularly to the imperial cult professing *Kaisar Soter*, "Caesar as Savior." Third, Paul comments on Christ's mystical cleansing of the church, which he makes "without a spot or wrinkle . . . holy and without blemish" (5:27). Such a bold image mimics the care and honor bestowed on a bride by her handmaidens as they prepare a bride for a wedding celebration. Fourth, Paul creates a vision of solace, comfort, and solicitude as Christ nourishes and cares for his bride even as a husband does for his own body (5:28–29).

The final description, and perhaps the most potent, hails Christ's union with his church even as a man leaves his parents and becomes one with his wife in physical union (5:31–32). To highlight this point, Paul employs yet again the word "mystery" to describe the multilayered nuances of Christ's intimate love, as he writes, "and the two will become one flesh. This is a great mystery, and I am applying it to Christ and the church" (5:31–32).[7] In essence, the union of Christ and his church mirrors a man and woman coming together in a lifelong commitment of marriage. As an impressionist painter adds brushstroke after brushstroke to create a vibrant montage of color, so the apostle creates a stunning portrait of Christ's profound love for his bride. Surely one of Paul's purposes in doing so is to urge the church to engage its role as the new humanity and become followers and lovers of Jesus, committed to the full expression of God's kingdom on Earth.

Scripture's Bridal Imagery

The concept of the *ecclesia* as the bride of Christ plays out well in Paul's mind as a Pharisee who understands the favored relationships of both Israel and the emerging church with the Father of Lights.[8] Also evident for him is that such bridal imagery is based upon scriptural allusions of God's passionate espoused love for Israel. Such bridal intimations are ample in

---

7. See Eph 3:1–13 for the reiterated use of *mystērion*.
8. Jas 1:17; Phil 3:4–6; see also Wright, "Three Worlds of Paul," in *Paul*, 3–13.

the discourse of the Prophets. Jeremiah speaks of Yahweh's passion when he pleads with Israel to repent, "Thus says the Lord: I remember the devotion of your youth, your love as a bride, how you followed me in the wilderness, in a land not sown" (Jer 2:2). Hosea reiterates the image with more graphic detail:

> Therefore, I will now persuade her, and bring her into the wilderness, and speak tenderly to her. From there I will give her her vineyards, and make the Valley of Achor a door of hope. There she shall respond as in the days of her youth, as at the time when she came out of the land of Egypt. On that day, says the Lord, you will call me, "My husband," and no longer will you call me, "My Baal." (Hos 2:14–16)

Again, Jeremiah describes the return of the exiles in terms of wedded love: "Thus says the Lord: . . . I have loved you with an everlasting love; therefore I have continued my faithfulness to you. Again I will build you, and you shall be built, O virgin Israel! Again you shall take your tambourines, and go forth in the dance of the merrymakers" (Jer 31:2–4). The prophet Ezekiel speaks of God's faithless bride: "I passed by you again and looked on you; you were at the age of love. I spread the edge of my cloak over you, and covered your nakedness: I pledged myself to you and entered into a covenant with you, says the Lord God, and you became mine" (Ezek 16:8).[9]

In the New Testament, we see further references of the *ecclesia* as both God's chosen people and as the bride of Christ. For example, Peter sings the praises of the nascent church in his well-known refrain, "But you are a chosen race, a royal priesthood, a holy nation, God's own people, in order that you may proclaim the mighty acts of him who called you out of darkness into his marvelous light" (1 Pet 2:9). As we have already noted, the apostle Paul describes the church as the bride of Christ and that as his bride the church belongs to him. "I feel a divine jealousy for you, for I promised you in marriage to one husband, to present you as a chaste virgin to Christ" (2 Cor 11:2), he writes to the Corinthian church. To the Roman Christians he explains, "In the same way, my friends, you have died to the law through the body of Christ, so that you may belong to another, to him who has been raised from the dead in order that we may bear fruit for God" (Rom 7:4). Again, to the Corinthians he writes, "Or do you not know that your body is a temple of the Holy Spirit within you, which you have from God, and that

---

9. See also Isa 54:1–6.

you are not your own. For you were bought with a price; therefore glorify God in your body" (1 Cor 6:19–20).

In the Gospels there are also a number of references to Jesus as the bridegroom, as when he speaks to his disciples about fasting: "The wedding-guests cannot mourn as long as the bridegroom is with them, can they? The days will come when the bridegroom is taken away from them, and then they will fast" (Matt 9:15).[10] It is apparent that God has a remarkable love for his chosen people, and such love is expressed through the cogent metaphor of wedded love. Abba loves his people as a husband loves his wife, and Christ reveals his intimate affection for his bride, the church of God.

The Heart of Desire

Abba desires to be in a relationship with every single person on Earth; he desires for everyone to respond to his overtures of love and to join the ranks of the people of God (1 Tim 2:3–4). He has created us and desires to know us in an intimate relationship, which implies that he desires a reciprocal loving response. As such, the purpose of our existence is to enter into a dynamic of love with our Creator God. Everything else is subservient to this fundamental invitation to intimacy. A beautiful passage that speaks to the theme of divine amity is the canticle of love found in the Song of Solomon:

> I slept, but my heart was awake. Listen! My beloved is knocking. "Open to me, my sister, my love, my dove, my perfect one; for my head is wet with dew, my locks with the drops of the night." I had put off my garment; how could I put it on again? I had bathed my feet; how could I soil them? My beloved thrust his hand into the opening, and my inmost being yearned for him. I arose to open to my beloved, and my hand dripped with myrrh, my fingers with liquid myrrh, upon the handles of the bolt. I opened to my beloved, but my beloved had turned and was gone. My soul failed me when he spoke. I sought him, but did not find him; I called him but he gave no answer. (Song 5:2–6)

As presented in this ode, the bride is ready for love but as she turns to embrace her lover she finds that he is gone. She calls out his name, searches for him, and implores others to find him but he is not to be found. As a bride, she eagerly waits for her marriage consummation, but the bridegroom has inexplicably vanished.

10. See also Mark 2:19–20; Luke 5:33–39; John 3:29–30.

The passion of the canticle surprisingly resonates with the Gospel story of Mary Magdalene coming to anoint the body of her Lord (John 20:1–18). Approaching the tomb, Mary finds the stone already moved to the side and the grave site empty. After alerting the disciples of the strange events, she stands before the tomb alone, weeping for her beloved Lord. Looking into it she sees two angels sitting where Jesus had lain who ask, "Woman, why are you weeping?" To their question, she flatly responds that the body of her Lord is missing and she has no idea where it has been taken. As she speaks, she turns and sees a man whom she assumes to be the gardener who similarly asks, "Woman, why are you weeping? Whom are you looking for?" To his query Mary answers, "Sir, if you have carried him away, tell me where you have laid him, and I will take him away" (John 20:11–17). Through Mary's dialogue and single-minded focus on her Lord, we find parallels with the longing presented in the Song of Songs. As the canticle's bride resolutely seeks her lover, so Mary desperately pines for Jesus. When he finally calls out her name, she rushes and clings to the feet of Christ. The texts converge as we observe in each story the passionate longing of the lover who desperately seeks a reunion with the beloved.

The Canadian poet Margaret Avison vividly reimagines the scene of Mary's passion for her Lord in her poem "Continued Story":

> What woman would not know?
>   He was gone.
> What woman would not try
> blindly every device—vigil
> by the night window, perfumes—
> before facing it? No
> lover beloved. Nobody.
>
> Cut off by stone?
> worse, cut off by
> no visible barrier:
> then all the more, her hope
> lay dying in her.

THE BRIDE OF CHRIST

> What woman would not
> scald her eye-sockets with those
> painful slow tears, largely unshed?
> to have lost even
> loss in an
> empty new day?
>
>> Whoever did this thing
>> is enemy: to me, now –
>> and to our friends. (She
>> claimed him still in her
>>> first person.)
>> Somebody may know something
>> someone can do, even now, even if
>> the authorities, having
>> acted the enemy, are
>> least of all to be trusted in this extremity.
>
> (He had purposed no riddle –
> 'Did I not tell you?')
>
>> **********
>
>> I don't know. But I saw,
>>> she cried. He told me to tell you ...
>
>> What woman, what man
>> dared believe her
>> here in enemy country?[11]

Both the scriptural passage and the poet's rendering speak to the shared desire between Christ and his bride, the church of God. It is not a long-distance relationship, or one which is defined by rules, regulations, or the

---

11. Avison, "Continued Story," in *Always Now*, 1:48–49.

characteristics of an institution. Rather, it is a passionate love affair between God and his people which is shown in a relationship of closeness. Along with God's other essential characteristics of compassion, forgiveness, and holiness, Philip Sheldrake speaks to the divine attribute of intimacy. Drawing on the insights of Julian of Norwich with her understanding of the idea of longing, he quotes the fourteenth-century mystic:

> "For as truly as there is in God a quality of pity and compassion, so truly is there in God a quality of thirst and longing: and the power of this longing in Christ enables us to respond to his longing, and without this no soul comes to heaven. And this quality of longing and thirst comes from God's everlasting goodness" (*Showings*, chapter 31).

Sheldrake concludes from Julian's observations, "God's fundamental desire is that we are to become united with God and to share in God's own 'bliss' . . . the quality of God's longing is not something accidental but is part of God's very nature from all eternity."[12]

It is this dimension of longing that is often lacking in our response to the heavenly overtures. We may intellectually believe that Abba longs for us, but we have not reciprocated with a corresponding intensity, perhaps because of the many challenges to our understanding and receptivity to Abba's divine overtures of love. For example, God is not experienced as a corporeal entity; from our sensorial awareness, he is invisible and seemingly unavailable. It calls for a measure of faith to respond to his embrace. Even more concerning, we sometimes offer a bored, lukewarm yawn unworthy of the God who is filled with passion and love (Rev 3:16). We fear losing control or giving ourselves over to a love which seems too demanding. Or we hold back, wondering about other possible love interests. Or we succumb to an apathetic malaise when it seems impossible to summon the desire for any passionate love. Such possibilities fail to understand the profundity of Abba's amazing love, which we have seen cannot be measured, and is as vast as a mighty river (Eph 3:18–19).

It is with this mystical God that we are invited to have a loving, intimate relationship through Jesus Christ. Helpfully, the singer of the Song of Songs leads us in the direction of God's passionate charity which is designed to fire all sectors of our lives:

---

12. Sheldrake, *Befriending Our Desires*, 39–40.

> Set me as a seal upon your heart, as a seal upon your arm; for love is as strong as death, passion fierce as the grave. Its flashes are flashes of fire, a raging flame. Many waters cannot quench love, neither can floods drown it. If one offered for love all the wealth of one's house, it would be utterly scorned. (Song 8:6–7)

In the book of Revelation the mystery finds resolution in John's portrayal of God coming down from heaven to dwell with his people on Earth. This movement is portrayed as the new Jerusalem descends to Earth:

> And I saw the holy city, the new Jerusalem, coming down out of heaven from God, prepared as a bride adorned for her husband. And I heard a loud voice from the throne saying, "See, the home of God is among mortals. He will dwell with them as their God, they will be his peoples, and God himself will be with them." (Rev 21:2–3)

Similar words are sounded to the Seer through the words of the angel, "'Come, I will show you the bride, the wife of the lamb.' And in the Spirit he carried me away to a great, high mountain and showed me the holy city Jerusalem coming down out of heaven from God" (21:10). On both occasions the aged apostle sees the holy city's descent from heaven as a bride prepared for her husband. It is striking to note that the entire scene is embedded with wedding imagery as it describes Abba's loving relationship with his people.[13] As a husband waits for the arrival of his beautiful bride, God is presented as a groom waiting for his bride, so that they might dwell together in bliss. Through John's apocryphal language we observe two images side by side: first, a depiction of the church as the bride of Christ; second, the city of Jerusalem descending to the Earth as the "wife of the Lamb" (21:10). The impact of the two panels is powerful as God is portrayed as a passionate lover—no longer invisible—receiving the bride of Christ in an intimate manner.

In light of the ongoing, downward movement of God, we return to self-reflection with some salient questions: Do we entertain a true desire for God? Do we want a God who comes down to us? Do we want his love or do we prefer to keep God at a distance? Do we turn aside for lesser, more tangible and manageable relationships and endeavors? Such questions highlight the importance of our response before our Creator and our responsibility for declaring our great yes to his loving overtures. The Seer of Revelation recognizes the importance of our longing for God and the

---

13. See Boring, *Revelation*, 222.

essential part we play in this relationship of intimacy. In his conclusion to his vision the writer says, "The Spirit and the bride say, 'Come.' And let everyone who hears say, 'Come.' And let everyone who is thirsty come. Let anyone who wishes take the water of life as a gift" (Rev 22:17). Through this threefold invitation, the writer calls for our intentional choice to enter into a passionate, loving relationship with our triune God. The potential for an inspiring love affair with the Father, Son, and Spirit awaits us.

Fuelling the Fires of Love

As one needs to remain close to a fire to feel its heat, so one needs to remain close to the fire of our triune God if we are to burn with spiritual ardor. Maintaining passion in any personal relationship takes time, effort, and above all, presence. The same thing is required if we are going to fire our passion for God. The question we all face is how do we intentionally pursue this life of love? A place to begin is to consider contemplative disciplines that help us develop a vibrant, spiritual life. The following suggestions are a way forward in shaping such a lifestyle.

To begin, a daily reading of the Scriptures is imperative for the renovation of our minds. There is a need to replace our old mental recordings of competition and comparison with new ones that lead us in the direction of Christ's healing love. This transference occurs as we bathe ourselves in the Scriptures. The enervating messages are replaced with the invigorating words of Abba's love. To this end it is helpful to spend some time each day in the reading, reflection, and comprehension of God's truth so that our minds are shaped in the ways of love.

Giving thanks to God on a daily basis is critical for the maintenance of our spiritual fervor. Gratitude funds the development of our interior health. It is so easy to adopt the world's attitude of "scarcity" when considering our own needs and the challenges that other people pose.[14] To counterbalance this negative weight we are invited to focus on the truth that the kingdom of God is characterized by abundance and not by scarcity. When Jesus provides food for the hungry crowds in the Gospels, he is demonstrating the kingdom characteristic of abundance (Mark 8:1–10, Matt 14:13–21). We are invited to give up our anxieties because we live with the assurance that Abba supplies our every need. Praise and gratitude become forms of spiritual therapy that raise us above the cultural

---

14. P. Palmer, *Active Life*, 124.

malaise and agitation that accost us at every turn, enabling us to rest in the sheltering arms of our Father God.

Silence before God allows for an opportunity to discern the Spirit's direction in our lives. The quantity of time depends on the individual but the practice of silence and solitude is imperative for the quieting of the world's incessant noise. We are called to be quiet and listen for God's healing and instructive voice as enjoined by the psalmist: "For God alone my soul waits in silence; from him comes my salvation" (Ps 62:1); similarly, "For God alone my soul waits in silence, for my hope is from him" (Ps 62:5). Even short periods of silence help in the centering process and aid in restoring a sense of equilibrium.

A regular practice of conversational prayer maintains spiritual vibrancy and deepens our spiritual well. As a friend shows interest in our daily experience, so Jesus wants to engage with us in the details of our lives. Some folk argue that the day-to-day routine is not worthy of Jesus' time, but that is not the picture presented in the Scriptures. As the author of 1 Peter notes, "Cast all your anxiety on him, because he cares for you" (1 Pet 5:7).[15] A love affair with Jesus is characterized by fluid and open communication. It is essential that we engage in this interior dialogue if we desire spiritual intimacy.

An openness to others in a spirit of empathy and charity increases our capacity for the spiritual life. Jesus is a compassionate Lord who is pleased with our own expressions of compassion for the hurting. If we are to grow in intimacy with Christ we must share his perspective of walking with the needy of the world.[16] Turning a blind eye to the exigencies of others reveals a lack of concern for the very ones that Christ esteems. As we look for opportunities to serve others, it draws us out of our safe world with its protective barriers and allows the Spirit of God to penetrate our hearts in fresh and powerful ways.

The ultimate tool for nurturing spiritual fervency is love. Paul makes this crystal clear in his First Letter to the Corinthians when he identifies love as the ultimate virtue of the Christian journey: "And now faith, hope and love abide, these three, and the greatest of these is love" (1 Cor 13:13). The fires of the spiritual life are fuelled as we live in love with all who cross our paths. It begins with our immediate family and extends to the community, neighborhood, workplace, and ultimately to the stranger

---

15. See also John 15:14.
16. Luke 10:29–37; Matt 25:31–46.

who briefly enters our lives. Love is what brings healing to the world and it is the fundamental force that binds our universe together. When we walk in its path we become God's face to others and most clearly imitate the Father of Lights (Eph 5:1–2).[17]

As the passionate bride of Christ we are called to receive and reflect Christ's overtures of love in the everyday of our lives. When we do this as a community of faith, a synergy of love is created and released through the interconnectedness of our gifts, talents, and zeal. Because of the compounding nature of our spiritual gifts, or *charisma*, it is critical that every person of the community be actively engaged in the body of Christ. When we join together as his passionate church, amazing things happen through the power of the Holy Spirit. Indeed, as Zechariah observes, insurmountable mountains are transformed into manageable plains, not by human ingenuity, but by the Spirit of our creative God (Zech 4:6). Eben Alexander points us in this direction as he reflects on his experience of passing into heaven amidst the trauma of a deep coma:

> Not only was my journey about love, but it was also about who we are and how connected we all are—the very meaning of all existence. I learned who I was up there, and when I came back, I realized that the last broken strands of who I am down here were sewn up. *You are loved.* Those words are what I needed to hear as an orphan, as a child who'd been given away. But it's also what every one of us in this materialistic age needs to hear as well . . . the unconditional love of our Creator.[18]

So it is that we are loved by God, both individually and as his people, the church, which the Seer acclaims as "the wife of the Lamb" (Rev 21:9). It is in this relationship of love that the central purpose of our lives is found, as we gratefully receive Christ's amity and as his bride return it, so that the entire Earth is enflamed with the fires of his love.

Questions for Reflection

1. The church as the bride of Christ is a powerful metaphor. What is your response to being Christ's beloved? How can this image become

---

17. See also Jas 1:27.
18. Alexander, *Proof of Heaven*, 170–71.

a funding source for your own spiritual journey as you contemplate Jesus' deep love for his bride?

2. Unfortunately, we often sterilize Christ's love by making it an abstraction or simply a vague idea. Such a perspective fails to recognize the passionate love that Jesus has for each of his followers. We are invited to dive into his deep river of love (Eph 3:14–21) and know on an experiential level the divine bliss. Such an experience is not meant to be relegated to the mystics like Julian of Norwich, Teresa of Ávila, Hildegard of Bingen, or John of the Cross, but is meant to be known by every believer. Through the coming week visualize yourself as being held in the arms of Christ and receiving his total love and acceptance.

3. Suggestions have been presented in this chapter for fueling the flames of love. Identify a few of the steps which resonate most with you and in an intentional manner implement these dimensions into your devotional regimen. As you do, reflect on your love relationship with Jesus and see if these adaptations support your relationship with him.

4. Eben Alexander experienced the love of God in a profound way in his journey throughout heaven. We also are able to travel with God through the gift of our imagination. For example, imagine yourself being held in his arms as he introduces you to the beauties and wonders of heaven. What vistas do you experience? How does this venture lead you deeper into his profound love? Spend some time journaling about Abba's love and the intimacy you experience as his bride.

11

Our Shadow Side

Ephesians 6:10–17

"Our capacity to choose changes constantly with our practice of life. The longer we continue to make the wrong decisions, the more our heart hardens; the more often we make the right decision, the more our heart softens—or better perhaps, comes alive."

Erich Fromm, The Heart of Man

"Finally, be strong in the Lord and in the strength of his power.
Put on the whole armor of God, so that you may be able to stand against the wiles of the devil.
    For our struggle is not against enemies of blood and flesh,
        but against the rulers,
            against the authorities,
                against the cosmic powers of this present
                darkness,
                    against the spiritual forces of evil
                    in the heavenly places.

Therefore take up **the whole armor of God,**
    so that you may be able to withstand on that evil day,
    and having done everything, to stand firm.

Stand therefore, and fasten the **belt of truth** *around your waist,*
    and put on the **breastplate of righteousness.**

*As **shoes** for your feet put on whatever will make you ready to proclaim **the gospel of peace**.*

*With all of these, take the **shield of faith**, with which you will be able to quench all the flaming arrows of the evil one.*

*Take the **helmet of salvation**,*
*and the **sword of the Spirit**, which is **the word of God**."*

(Ephesians 6:10–17)

As we have seen, we are invited to embrace the passionate love that God has for his beloved bride. Paradoxically, as we are drawn towards Abba's loving overtures, there remains a part of ourselves that resists his love. Henri Nouwen notes this internal tension: "We are so resistant to listen to that [God's] voice, because partially we want it, and in part, we don't. Partially we want someone to love us, but we also don't want people or God to say things we don't want to hear. So there is as much desire for God as resistance against God."[1] This resistance (or our shadow side) represents the interior battle of wanting to know God and yet, simultaneously, seeking our own interests and self-centered desires. It is to this interior struggle that Paul turns as he draws his letter to a close. He is well aware that the journey to the true self is not attained without significant effort, intentionality, and perseverance. The apostle alludes to this journey towards wholeness in his correspondence to the Philippian community, as he urges them to "work out your own salvation with fear and trembling" (Phil 2:12). Such a journey is not for the faint of heart; rather it is an invitation to plumb the depths of Abba's love, which is "as fierce as death" (Song 8:6) and face the shadows that lurk within and the monsters that rage without.

The Reality of Evil

Paul lived in an age that accepted the veracity of personal evil, so it is not surprising that Paul underscores to the church that "our struggle is not against enemies of blood and flesh, but against the rulers, against the

---

1. Roderick, *Beloved*, 42.

authorities, against the cosmic powers of this present darkness, against the spiritual forces of evil in the heavenly places" (Eph 6:12). The apostle is not hesitant to name evil as evil and begins his description with the declaration that evil is powerful.[2] To this end he employs a variety of power words including "rulers," "authorities," "cosmic powers"—literally, "world rulers"—and "forces of evil"— literally, "evil spirits." For Paul, evil is not an innocuous abstraction like a theme for contemporary video games, but speaks to powerful forces that fight against the establishment of God's kingdom. Jesus portrays a similar worldview when he refers to Satan as "the ruler of this world" (John 12:31) and the writer of 1 John highlights "that the whole world lies under the power of the evil one" (5:19). Jesus stresses that God is ultimately in control and that evil is no match for God's power (Matt 16:18), but at the same time maleficent forces must be recognized as consequential challenges in one's journey of faith. C.S. Lewis is helpful on this point as he provides instructive commentary on how to maintain a cogent understanding of evil without being overwhelmed by it:

> There are two equal and opposite errors into which our race can fall about the devils. One is to disbelieve in their existence. The other is to believe, and to feel an excessive and unhealthy interest in them. They themselves are equally pleased by both errors and hail a materialist or a magician with the same delight.[3]

We are to acknowledge the reality of evil without being derailed by it; at the same time, we are not to exaggerate the demonic presence so that we imagine demons to be hiding under every bush!

A second characteristic of evil is that the powers are wicked.[4] Paul identifies this malfeasance through the terms "present darkness" and "the spiritual forces of evil" and argues that these agencies use their powers for the purpose of destruction. Jesus identifies a number of ways that the evil one works havoc in our world. He is known as "the tempter" (Matt 4:3), steering individuals in directions of weakness contrary to spiritual growth; "the accuser" (Rev 12:10), bringing charges against believers (and before God) leading to discouragement; and as "a liar" (John 8:44), deceiving and dividing the church of Christ. Richard Lovelace underscores the evil one's *modus operandi*:

---

2. Stott, *God's New Society*, 263.
3. Lewis, *Screwtape Letters*, 13.
4. Stott, *God's New Society*, 264.

> The devil lives in a universe of deception. This is part of the reason his legions are called "powers of darkness" . . . just as in any efficient dictatorship, the devil seeks to control the media. He seeks to block the broadcast of truth, and to insert and energize whatever is morally degrading and conducive to unbelief.[5]

The devil is not only the tempter, accuser, and liar, but he operates as the oppressor, promoting systems of tyranny, injustice, brutality, and violence, all with the endgame of benefiting a few at the expense of the general populous.[6] Evil seeks destruction and uses individuals, institutions, structures, and corporations as tools for the undermining of culture and the degradation of the planet.

Third, when Paul speaks of "the wiles of the devil" (Eph 6:11), he is calling our attention to the powers as cunning.[7] The word the apostle employs for "wiles" is *methodeia*, which includes "schemings, craftiness, wiles, stratagems."[8] It addresses capacities such as intelligence, astuteness, reflection, and planning—all employed for the destruction of humanity. As we look at our world, evil is readily seen through a pandemic of wars, injustice, sexual exploitation, pollution, climatic degradation, racism, and tribalism. Often it is not identified as "personal evil" but its existence is apparent and the majority of faith traditions acknowledge it. The battleground is fought on two fronts—planet Earth at large and the individual human heart and mind. Destruction is evidenced on a planetary scale through war, genocide, slavery, razing of the forests, and despoiling of the oceans; it is seen in the individual's interior world through addictions, bondage, oppression, and deception. As in Mary Shelley's novel *Frankenstein*, we have helped to create a monster and its desire is to destroy everything that we love. It does not serve us well to deny the reality of evil or pretend it does not exist. Rather, we are invited to meet it head on, and as "overcomers" undo it through the power of our conquering Lord (1 John 5:5 NIV).

A Call to Stand

In the book of Joshua there is an intriguing story in which Joshua encounters an unknown soldier dressed for battle. It takes place in the days preceding

---

5. Lovelace, *Renewal as a Way of Life*, 108.
6. See Lovelace, *Renewal as a Way of Life*, 105–8, on the devil's strategies.
7. See Stott, *God's New Society*, 264–65.
8. Kubo, *Reader's Greek-English Lexicon*, 187.

Israel's assault on Jericho so he is keenly interested in the allegiance of this curious soldier. Joshua approaches the unknown soldier and directly asks him, "Are you one of us, or one of our adversaries?," to which the soldier responds, "Neither; but as commander of the army of the Lord I have now come." In response to this revelation Joshua falls to his knees in worship and asks, "What do you command your servant, my lord?" To this question the commander orders Joshua to remove his sandals for the place where he stands is holy (Josh 5:13–15). In this narrative God is presented as a warrior who stands with his people and fights against the forces of evil. Through it we are reminded that Yahweh is with us as we face the challenges and difficulties of life and empowers us as we battle in this present darkness.

In a similar manner, Paul encourages the Ephesians that God enables them to not only face evil but repel its onslaughts. The key idea in dealing with the devil's strategies is contained in his imperative *histēmi*, "to stand": "Therefore take up the whole armor of God, so that you may be able to withstand on that evil day, and having done everything, to stand firm" (Eph 6:13). Indeed, Paul reiterates this point on four occasions to focus on the believer's stability as he or she faces the wiles of the evil one (5:11, 13, 14). Our standing depends upon our roots growing deep into the soil of God's living and written Word so that we are not "tossed to and fro" by evil's "trickery, craftiness and deceitful scheming" (4:14). The same truth is underscored in the wisdom literature of Proverbs: "the root of the righteous will never be moved" (Prov 12:3); "the root of the righteous bears fruit" (12:12); and "When the tempest passes, the wicked are no more, but the righteous are established for ever" (10:25). In each of these references the depiction is of strength, stability, perseverance, and fortitude even within the topsy-turvy experience of the spiritual journey. Paul does not insist on heroic action or mighty deeds of valor; we do not need to be like Don Quixote charging windmills erroneously perceived as evil giants![9] Rather, he encourages us to stand our ground in the power of God and trust the Holy Spirit to work through us for the Father's glory. It is an act of humility to stand in dependence and wait upon God's direction even as the children of Israel waited upon the Lord to part the waters and enabled their escape from the pursuing armies of Pharaoh.

We stand our ground by putting on the armor of God, Paul writes from prison (Eph 3:1). The constant presence of a guard dressed for action becomes a model, a vivid image, for the apostle to explain the availability

---

9. Cervantes, *Don Quixote*, 65–67.

of divine protection. Paul is direct: "Therefore take up the whole armor of God" (6:13); even as the prophet Isaiah depicted God wearing armor in his fight against wickedness: "Righteousness shall be the belt around his waist, and faithfulness the belt around his loins" (Isa 11:4–5).[10] Paul promotes a complementary image in his Letter to the Romans as he exhorts the faith community to "lay aside the works of darkness and put on the armor of light" (Rom 13:12). For Paul, the church needs to be vigilant in recognizing the ploys of the evil one and determined to resist his tactics by taking up the provision of God's armor on a daily basis. Covert fascination with evil leads to disaster as one's personal resistance is no match for the prince of this world. As the poet of the Canticles avers, we are to "catch the foxes, the little foxes that ruin the vineyard" (Song 2:15) and not allow our proclivities to run rampant and bring about our spiritual demise.

Putting on the Armor of God

The Belt of Truth

Paul begins his sixfold description of the armor of God with the belt of truth (Eph 6:14). As Muddiman suggests, the belt has allusions to both "the oriental flowing robes need[ing] to be hitched up for ease of movement" and the belt used by the Roman soldier to hold the leather apron or sword belt in place.[11] Paul has spoken previously of the importance of the "word of truth" (1:13) which the Ephesians had heard and believed in, and that ultimate truth is found in the person of Jesus (4:21). He has further encouraged the community to put on "true righteousness" (4:24) and to "speak the truth" to one another and to their Gentile neighbors (4:25). Truth is to be an essential characteristic of the new humanity, which contrasts with the deception of the evil one and the practice of falsehood commonly demonstrated throughout society.

For Paul, faith is shaped by a renewing of one's mind through the renovating work of the Holy Spirit, entailing a "putting off of the old mind" and a "putting on of the new mind" in Christ (Col 3:2, 9, 10). The apostle speaks of this exchange in his Letter to the Romans: "To set the mind on the flesh is death, but to set the mind on the Spirit is life and peace" (Rom 8:6); and "Do not be conformed to this world, but be transformed by the renewing of

---

10. See also Isa 52:7; 59:17.
11. Muddiman, *Epistle to the Ephesians*, 290.

your minds, so that you may discern what is the will of God—what is good and acceptable and perfect (Rom 12:2). We also note that Jesus describes the faith journey as a life of truth and freedom when he encourages his listeners with the affirmations that "the truth will make you free" (John 8:23) and that "I am the way, and the truth, and the life" (John 14:6).

The crux of the matter, as Wright reminds us, is that the gospel is meaningless if it is not true.[12] If it is true it becomes our source for empowerment and the key for living the abundant life.[13] We are invited to receive the truth and to allow it to penetrate our minds to our very core. This happens as we bathe ourselves in God's word and allow the Scriptures to transform our thinking patterns, which ultimately leads to a change in behavior. Daily reading of the Word reshapes our minds so that the truth of God molds our decision-making rather than the mores of our culture. Memorizing the Word is also beneficial, for as we turn the words of Scripture over in our minds the world's competitive messages are replaced by the comforting words of Abba's love and grace. These truths work on a subterranean level in both our consciousness and unconsciousness, reshaping our new lives in Christ. Therefore, it is essential that we consider what we are putting into our minds, so that, as Henri Nouwen says, "we are not walking around with a garbage can on our heads," taking in whatever the world is offering.[14] Rather, each day we invite the Spirit to pour into our lives through a practice of spiritual reading—Scripture, spiritual books, music, videos—so that we are fortified as God's daughters and sons. By doing so we guard our minds and hearts and do not give the evil one an opportunity for gaining a foothold in our lives (Eph 4:27).

The Breastplate of Righteousness

The second piece of armor Paul identifies is "the breastplate of righteousness" (Eph 6:14). In prophetic literature the breastplate of righteousness refers to God's desire for justice and his inveterate effort to release the oppressed from their task masters. Isaiah recounts,

> The Lord saw it, and it displeased him that there was no justice.
> He saw that there was no one, and was appalled that there was

---

12. Wright, *Paul for Everyone*, 74.
13. See John 7:38; Matt 25:29; Rom 5:17.
14. Roderick, *Beloved*, 18.

no one to intervene; so his own arm brought him victory, and his righteousness upheld him. He put on righteousness like a breastplate, and a helmet of salvation on his head; he put on garments of vengeance for clothing, and wrapped himself in fury as in a mantle. (Isa 59:15–17)

Building on this prophetic foundation, Paul constructs a two-pronged argument for the importance of righteousness in the believer's life. First, "righteousness" refers to God's righteousness, which is applied to the believer through the sacrificial work of Christ. We see this sense of the word in Paul's previous writings. To the Roman Christians he explains, "For I am not ashamed of the gospel; it is the power of God for salvation to everyone who has faith, to the Jew first and also to the Greek. For in it the righteousness of God is revealed through faith for faith; as it is written, 'The one who is righteous will live by faith'" (Rom 1:16–17). He explains to the Galatians, "For through the Spirit, by faith, we eagerly wait for the hope of righteousness" (Gal 5:5). God sees us as righteous and pure though the lens of Jesus Christ as we come into a relationship with his Son. Paul emphasizes the same truth by employing the word "salvation" as a synonym for righteousness in this Ephesian epistle: "For by grace you have been saved through faith, and this is not your own doing; it is the gift of God—not the result of works, so that no one may boast" (Eph 2:8–9).

Second, the believer has a heartfelt desire for the characteristic of righteousness as a follower of Jesus. Paul underscores this dimension by encouraging the believer to "clothe yourselves with the new self . . . in true righteousness and holiness" (4:24) and also by demonstrating the threefold fruit of "goodness, righteousness, and truth" (5:9). As we pursue our imitation of the Father (5:1–2) there is an honest desire for righteous living. Nothing helps us more in this regard than bearing "the weapons of righteousness for the right hand and for the left," as Paul poetically pens (2 Cor 6:7).

Righteousness is not shown in anger or an attitude of moral superiority; rather, it is a demonstration of Abba's compassionate love towards the hurting and marginalized of our world. This disposition of love is an essential component of the church as it seeks to work for justice and bring God's goodness to bear in a world characterized by a me-first mentality. A beautiful picture of this humble righteousness is depicted in the Lord of the Rings trilogy by Frodo on his quest to Mount Doom as he travels with the rest of the Fellowship to destroy the ring of Sauron. Throughout the journey he wears Bilbo's undergarment of Elven chainmail as a protective shield for his diminutive hobbit body. During a battle in the mines of Moria he is speared by an Orc chieftain and left for dead. After the Fellowship finally defeats the Orcan regiment and returns to Frodo, he appears to have died in battle from the thrust of a spear. Upon closer examination they discover that the sword has not penetrated the Elven chainmail and that Frodo, although severely bruised, is still alive![15] In a similar way, the righteousness of Abba protects us from the onslaught of evil with its nefarious configurations of wickedness, deception, and temptation. Hence, it remains critical, as Paul enjoins, to put the breastplate on and to experience its protection in the everyday of our pilgrimage of faith.

The Shoes of Peace

Third, Paul invites us to put on shoes that enable us to proclaim the gospel of peace (Eph 6:15). Once again Paul finds his inspiration from the voice of the prophets, as Isaiah writes, "How beautiful upon the mountains are the feet of the messenger who announces peace, who brings good news, who announces salvation, who says to Zion, 'Your God reigns'" (Isa 52:7). Paul himself repeats the prophet's words in his Letter to the Romans (10:15). The believer is to dress for the long march by putting on sandals or boots and be ready to communicate the values of the kingdom as the opportunities arise. Preparing the feet for engagement alludes to the forward movement of the gospel as believers go out in mission sharing the story of God's amazing grace. Jesus alludes to this missional dimension when he prepares the twelve disciples for their evangelistic sojourns, instructing them to "wear sandals" (Mark 6:9) and encouraging them to share peace with all the homes that receive them (Matt 10:13). The references to sandals and sharing peace by both Jesus and Paul remind the believing community that mission and vocation are essential ingredients for the Christian journey. Life is not simply about climbing the ladder of success or pursuing endless entertainment; rather, it involves living authentically so that the gospel light shines within a wanting world.[16] For Paul, the leading edge of this mission is to work for peace and reconciliation, so that Jews and Gentiles are brought into unity as God's new humanity. Christ is our peace and this truth is to be demonstrated as the church pursues rapprochement

---

15. The description is based on the scene from the film *The Lord of the Rings*, directed by Peter Jackson, based on Tolkien's story from *The Fellowship of the Rings*.

16. See Dawn, *Unfettered Hope*, 195–96.

rather than enmity. Reconciliation is not simply a theory or an idea but represents a sustained effort to overcome any estrangement or alienation with the compassionate love of Jesus.[17] A tangible example within our own milieu is Tyndale Seminary's partnership with the North America Institute for Indigenous Theological Studies (NAIITS), offering a master's degree in indigenous studies to further one's understanding between the church and the indigenous community, culture, and praxis.[18]

The Shield of Faith

Before we consider the "shield of faith" as a part of God's panoply (Eph 6:16), it is important to note the essential role that faith plays in the life of the community. Paul first mentions the dimension of faith in his greetings (Eph 1:1) and in his commendation concerning the community's commitment to Christ, "I have heard of your faith in the Lord Jesus and your love toward all the saints" (1:15). Subsequently, he affirms the crucial step of being receptive to the Spirit's drawings and of coming to Christ through faith: "For by grace you have been saved through faith, and this is not your own doing; it is the gift of God" (2:8). Paul proceeds to detail the import of embracing the "unity of [in] the faith" while advancing in spiritual maturity (4:13). In our immediate text, Paul encourages the Ephesians to wield "the shield of faith" (6:16), alluding to both salvation through faith and the expression of a faithful Christian witness. As Paul closes his letter he references Tychicus as "a faithful minister in the Lord" (6:21) and in his final benediction prays for peace, love, faith (6:23), and grace for the church of Christ.

Returning to the armor of God, we note that the fourth piece of defense the believer takes up is "the shield of faith" (6:16). The specific shield Paul identifies is "a full-length shield of leather-covered wood that protect[s] the whole body" and was employed to protect the soldier from fiery projectiles and sword strikes experienced during hand-to-hand combat.[19] In the film *Gladiator* there is a fine example of the shield's deployment when Maximus, the former general turned gladiator, trains his fellow combatants to use their Roman shields as a defense strategy against the spikes of the chariot wheels, providing them time and space to gain the upper hand

17. Eph 3:18–19; 1 Tim 2:4; Heb 2:9; 2 Pet 3:9. See also Pinnock, *Grace Unlimited*.
18. See https://www.tyndale.ca/seminary/study/mts-indiginous-studies.
19. Perkins, *Ephesians*, 146–47.

amidst their adversaries. As we have seen, Paul bases his description of God's armor on Old Testament texts, in this case, passages identifying God as a Guardian for his people: "Do not be afraid, Abram, I am your shield; your reward shall be great" (Gen 15:1); "This God—his way is perfect; the promise of the Lord proves true; he is a shield for all who take refuge in him" (Ps 18:30); "For you bless the righteous, O Lord; you cover them with favor as with a shield" (Ps 5:12); "The Lord is my strength and my shield; in him my heart trusts; so I am helped, and my heart exults, and with my song I give thanks to him" (Ps 28:7).

The specific function that Paul identifies for "the shield of faith" is its ability to "quench all the flaming arrows of the evil one" (Eph 6:16). The fiery darts come through an array of accusations and deception that the devil casts upon the believer, including temptations, lies, false guilt, fear, lust, doubts, and spiritual attacks bearing misfortune, sickness, and pain.[20] The writer of 1 Peter concurs with Paul's understanding regarding the sanctuary of faith: "Discipline yourselves, keep alert. Like a roaring lion your adversary the devil prowls around, looking for someone to devour. Resist him, steadfast in your faith, for you know that your brothers and sisters in all the world are undergoing the same kinds of suffering" (1 Peter 5:8–9). In this light it is imperative that we maintain our faith in Jesus if we are to stand firm and overcome the attacks of the evil one.

In *The Pilgrim's Progress* John Bunyan tells the story of Christian facing Apollyon in the Valley of Humiliation. The monster "threw a flaming dart at his breast; but Christian had a shield in his hand, with which he caught it, and so prevented the danger of that."[21] As Bunyan's Christian models for us, we must be ready to resist the wiles of the devil for he is a formidable foe! We will not stand if we are unprepared or cling to the ways of the false self. Rather, we must put on the new self and live out our every day in the confidence of Christ's sheltering presence.

---

20. See Wright, *Paul for Everyone*, 74–75, for further commentary on the devil's fiery arrows.

21. Bunyan, *Pilgrim's Progress*, 59. In that dramatic scene with Apollyon, Christian needs all the armor, and particularly the sword and shield together, to finally escape "the foul fiend."

The Helmet of Salvation and the Sword of the Spirit

Paul further encourages the Ephesians to don "the helmet of salvation" (Eph 6:17), which is an allusion to the Roman helmet made of iron or bronze. Marcus Barth adds the interesting fact that the helmet had "a lining of felt or sponge to make the weight bearable."[22] Isaiah's description of God's armor includes the helmet: "He put on righteousness like a breastplate, and a helmet of salvation on his head" (Isa 59:17). We also observe that Paul alludes to the helmet in his Thessalonian correspondence: "But since we belong to the day, let us be sober, and put on the breastplate of faith and love, and for a helmet the hope of salvation" (1 Thess 5:8). For Paul, the "helmet of salvation" has a twofold focus: first, it addresses the believer's current standing and acceptance before God based on the salvific work of Christ—"even when we were dead through our trespasses, [God] made us alive together with Christ—by grace you have been saved" (Eph 2:5); second, it speaks of eternal salvation which one receives as a "gift from [of] God" (2:8). Donning "the helmet of salvation" reassures the Christian that victory over the evil one is certain due to God's provision that is found in Jesus Christ.[23] As a result, we do not have to keep questioning our salvation. Abba has worked in Jesus to supply all of our needs, as Paul writes elsewhere, "And my God will fully satisfy every need of yours according to his riches in glory in Christ Jesus" (Phil 4:19). This most certainly includes for his children eternal standing through faith in Jesus Christ as Lord.

With the helmet of salvation we are to engage the final piece of armor, which is the *machaira*, or "short sword," used in hand-to-hand combat (Eph 6:17). As in the other cases, the allusion to the sword is based on God's armor, as Isaiah references: "but with righteousness he shall judge the poor, and decide with equity for the meek of the earth; he shall strike the earth with the rod of his mouth, and with the breath of his lips he shall kill the wicked" (Isa 11:4). Again, "He made my mouth like a sharp sword, in the shadow of his hand he hid me; he made me a polished arrow, in his quiver he hid me away" (49:2). The apostle qualifies the sword as "the sword of the Spirit which is the word of God" (Eph 6:17), clearly linking it with both the Spirit and God's word. Having identified the offensive nature of the *machaira*, Paul elaborates on the benefits the believer accrues by its deployment. First, "the sword" provides a sense of hope as the

---

22. Barth, *Ephesians*, 2:775.
23. Muddiman, *Epistle to the Ephesians*, 293.

indwelling Spirit transmits an understanding of one's acceptance before the Father. Paul has noted earlier, "And do not grieve the Holy Spirit of God, with which you were marked with a seal for the day of redemption" (Eph 4:30), and "In him you also, when you had heard the word of truth, the gospel of your salvation, and had believed in him, were marked with the seal of the promised Holy Spirit" (1:13).[24]

Second, the sword as "the word of God" establishes a position of readiness as the believer enters into the foray against evil. The word provides a stable foundation for battle which serves as a counterpoint for "being tossed about by [the] waves of doubt" (4:14) and is masterfully exemplified by Jesus as he overcomes the devil's temptations in the wilderness through the use of Scripture (Matt 4:4, 8, 11). Third, the sword as God's word contains a juridical quality which convicts and reproves individuals drawing them to God in a spirit of repentance.[25] The author of Hebrews addresses this specific point, explaining, "Indeed, the word of God is living and active, sharper than any two-edged sword, piercing until it divides soul from spirit, joints from marrow; it is able to judge the thoughts and intentions of the heart" (Heb 4:12). Fourth, the word of God under the direction of the Holy Spirit changes lives through the proclamation of the gospel, in both "conversion through belief" (Rom 10:8) and "righteousness through good deeds" (Jas 1:22–27; 2:14–26).

In sum, the sword, as it is linked with the Spirit and the word of God, is transformed into a crucial piece of armor which one brandishes in the battle with wickedness. As C. S. Lewis presents Peter, with sword in hand, leading the citizens of Narnia into battle with the nefarious witch in *The Lion, the Witch, and the Wardrobe*, so it is essential that as followers of Jesus we take up the "sword of the Spirit" to stand against the strategies and deceptive methodologies of the evil one.[26]

Going Forth in the Armor of Light

God provides the armor for resisting and overcoming iniquity, but to be successful we must put the armor on! We are not to dally with compulsive behaviors but be diligent in saying no to our destructive patterns. We must be tenacious in clothing ourselves with the armor of light (Rom 13:12).

---

24. See also Col 3:3.
25. See Muddiman, *Epistle to the Ephesians*, 294.
26. Lewis, *Lion, the Witch, and the Wardrobe*, 193–94.

As we do so, we gain the confidence that we have the necessary means to conquer the wiles of the devil and to live victoriously as Abba's children. In knowing that evil has been overcome through the downward way of the cross, we are able to stop playing the role as the devil's peon (Col 2:13–15). In light of this transformation there is an increasing desire to make choices that lead us into a deeper relationship with Jesus. Instead of giving into the egocentric desires of the false self, we break through its power by putting on the true self of Christ's compassionate love.[27] Indeed, our true longing becomes the affirmation of liberty and advancement in the pilgrimage of faith. We reiterate our yes by folding back into Jesus, as branches weave in and out of the vine (John 15:4–5). As we live in such a manner we experience the strength, support, and power of the authentic life and are not dismayed by the enervating snares of destructive living.

Paul emphasizes that we are to stand our ground in Christ (Eph 6:11, 13, 14) while being alert, attentive, and dependent upon the Spirit of God. We understand that spiritual attacks take place. If we persist in donning the armor of light, our standing is firm and evil does not overcome us.[28] This standing becomes our habitual experience as we open our hands and hearts to the ongoing filling of the Holy Spirit (Eph 5:18) and are receptive to the Spirit's guidance in living out our every day (Gal 5:25). The verb *plēroō*, "to fill," is in the present-passive-imperative, which speaks to a continual openness and filling by the Holy Spirit. As John Stott emphasizes, "For the fullness of the Spirit is not a once-for-all experience which we can never lose, but a privilege to be renewed continuously by continuous believing and obedient appropriation."[29] For Paul, a lifestyle of being filled with the Spirit is characterized by actions of worship —"sing psalms, hymns and spiritual songs" (5:19); active engagement in communal living—"among yourselves" (5:19); the expression of joy through a spirit of gratitude—"giving thanks to God the Father at all times" (5:20); and an awareness of Abba's presence in all dimensions of life—"for everything" (5:20).

As we put on the armor of light we are actually putting on Christ. We are clothing ourselves with his righteousness, peace, faith, fortitude, and salvation—all gifts that he provides through his victory on the cross. Paul understands that these virtues are bound together by divine love (Col 3:14) which rains down from above and "into our hearts through the Holy

---

27. McNeill et al., *Compassion*, 37.
28. Wright, *Paul for Everyone*, 76.
29. Stott, *God's New Society*, 209.

Spirit" (Rom 5:5). God's armor is ultimately the love of Christ that protects and enables us to overcome the destructive strategies of the evil one. As a result, we are secure in our identity as his daughters and sons because, as Brueggemann advises, we know "who we are" and "whose we are" through the demonstration of Abba's love.[30] Claiming our identity engenders a sense of confidence as we embrace our vocation in God's kingdom and complete the good works that he has established for us (Eph 2:10). For this reason, it is imperative that we stay rooted in his love so that we remain healthy and fruitful in our every day.

Notwithstanding, it is often during the times of trial that we experience the greatest advancement in our spiritual journey, even as Christ launched his ministry after being tempted in the wilderness (Luke 4:1–19). It is self-evident that we learn much about ourselves as we face our weaknesses and attempt to navigate life's turbulent waters. As we gain the insight of not depending on our own capabilities but trusting in Christ's indwelling presence, we increase in confidence through the Spirit's empowerment. Paul reminds us that "the weapons of our warfare are not merely human, but they have divine power to destroy strongholds. We destroy arguments and every proud obstacle raised up against the knowledge of God, and we take every thought captive to obey Christ" (2 Cor 10:4–5). It is this remarkable vision that Paul encourages us to embrace as the bride of Christ, for as we know the assurance of belonging to Jesus (2 Cor 10:7) we understand that nothing can undo Christ's passionate love or thwart our journey to love's consummation.

Questions for Reflection

1. Henri Nouwen observes that the Christian both desires and resists God. In your own life how do you relate to this dynamic of both seeking and turning away from Abba? Spend some time journaling about possible ways to resolve this dilemma.

2. Paul argues that throughout our spiritual journey we wrestle against spiritual powers. In what way do you identify "spiritual forces of evil" and how are they manifested in your everyday life?

3. Putting on the panoply of God enables us to stand our ground against the wiles of the evil one. As you reflect upon God's armor consider

---

30. Brueggemann, *Finally Comes the Poet*, 121.

which pieces are most helpful as you continue your spiritual pilgrimage. In your journal comment on how these pieces support you in your battle with evil.

4. Making positive choices that keep us away from spiritually dark places is crucial if we are to live with confidence and fortitude. Are there areas in your life where improved choices would help clear the spiritual clutter and energize your walk with Jesus? Share your challenges with a soul friend and together ask the Holy Spirit for guidance in overcoming spiritual deception and oppression.

12

Going Deeper

Ephesians 6:18–24

"Our real problem, in failing to center down, is not a lack of time; it is, I fear, in too many of us, lack of joyful, enthusiastic delight in Him, lack of deep, deep-drawing love directed toward Him at every hour of the day and night."

Thomas Kelly, A Testament of Devotion

"Music and silence—how I detest them both! . . . We will make the whole universe a noise in the end. We have already made great strides in this direction as regards the Earth. The melodies and silences of Heaven will be shouted down in the end."

Screwtape's threat, C. S. Lewis, The Screwtape Letters

"Pray in the Spirit at all times in every prayer and supplication.
To that end keep alert and always persevere in supplication for all the saints.
Pray also for me,
> *so that when I speak, a message may be given to me to make known*
> *with boldness the mystery of the gospel,*
>> *for which I am an ambassador in chains.*
> *Pray that I may declare it boldly, as I must speak.*

So that you may also know how I am and what I am doing,
> *Tychicus will tell you everything.*
> *He is a dear brother and a faithful minister in the Lord.*

GOING DEEPER

I am sending him to you for this very purpose,
to let you know how we are, and to encourage your hearts.

Peace be to the whole community, and love with faith,
from God the Father and the Lord Jesus Christ.

Grace be with all who have an undying love for our Lord Jesus Christ."
(Ephesians 6:18–24)

Diving in the waters of Saba presents its own challenges and rewards. Since these dives are routinely in deep waters with unaided descents of over one hundred feet, the adventure begins with the depths and dramatic descents. The most celebrated dive sites are "the pinnacles," which are seamounts rising up from the ocean floor, and the *pièce de résistance* is "the needle." This unique pinnacle rises from the ocean depths as a great spire, narrowing as an upside-down spike, while the surface beckons in the distance. To dive the pinnacle, one makes an open blue descent of over one hundred feet before encountering the encrusted volcanic formation. The diver is greeted by a montage of corals, sponges, and sea fans providing shelter for a diverse ensemble of groupers, parrot fish, butterfly fish, angel fish, green turtles, and blacktip sharks. It is an exhilarating dive site, but it is only enjoyed by those who are willing to penetrate the deep blue and expend the effort in reaching an elusive oceanic gem.

Similarly, Paul invites us to dive deep into our relationship with the Divine Family. It is a daunting challenge, but if we embrace it we experience the ultimate reward of becoming a true friend of Jesus. C. S. Lewis describes both the demands and rewards of the journey as he paraphrases the teaching of Jesus (see Matt 5:48):

> Make no mistake, if you let me, I will make you perfect. The moment you put yourself in My hands, that is what you are in for. Nothing less, or other, than that. You have free will, and if you choose, you can push Me away. But if you do not push Me away, understand that I am going to see this job through.[1]

---

1. Lewis, *Mere Christianity*, 202.

Perfection refers to the process of becoming a fully integrated person; that is, conforming to the mores of Jesus, and as a result experiencing his joy, peace, and compassionate love. It is towards this horizon that Paul sails, encouraging us to penetrate the deep waters of Jesus and to find our shelter in his loving arms.

Deeper into Prayer

Paul closes his letter by looking backward and forward as he encourages the church "to pray in the Spirit at all times in every prayer and supplication" (Eph 6:18). Casting towards the rear, he links his exhortation on spiritual warfare with the dynamic of prayer as it supports one in the fight against evil.[2] Looking ahead, he insists that prayer is the lifeblood of the community as it becomes the conduit for the Spirit's ongoing work. Highlighting its importance Paul connects the descriptor "all" to the action of prayer, as seen in "all times," "all prayers," "with all perseverance," and for "all the saints." Regretfully, as John Stott observes, it is not unusual in our day to substitute the injunction "all" with the more *laissez-faire* practice of "some," as in "sometimes," "some prayers," "some perseverance," and "for some saints."[3] Paul's linkage of "prayer" and "the Spirit" (6:18) is a constant theme for the apostle, as he demonstrates in some of his other writings: "Likewise the Spirit helps us in our weakness; for we do not know how to pray as we ought, but that very Spirit intercedes with sighs too deep for words" (Rom 8:26); "pray without ceasing, give thanks in all circumstances; for this is the will of God in Christ for you. Do not quench the Spirit" (1 Thess 5:17–19). By tethering prayer to the Spirit, a dynamic relationship is presented in which the totality of life is touched by the divine presence, as the apostle notes in "pray[ing] at all times," "for all the saints," and "pray also for me" (6:18–19). This interplay unfolds as we gather the disparate pieces of our lives and offer its entirety to the creative work of the Spirit. Practically this takes place through the ongoing discipline of "living prayer" in which nothing is excluded from prayer's penetrating touch.[4]

Pursuing this path of integration, we live with awareness and remain alert to the movement of the Holy Spirit in our lives. The call for being

---

2. See Luke 22:3, 53; 11:40, 46.

3. Stott, *God's New Society*, 283.

4. On "living prayer" see passages such as 1 Thess 5:16–18; Phil 4:6–7; Col 4:2; Eph 6:18.

"alert" and "always persever[ing]" highlights the significance of being attentive to the Spirit's breath in our everyday world. This practice follows Jesus's command to his disciples to "keep watch" and "pray" as observed during his turmoil in Gethsemane (Mark 14:32–42). We also hear Paul's allusion to this practice in his recitation of the baptismal creed, "Sleeper, awake! Rise from the dead, and Christ will shine on you" (Eph 5:14). Lamentably, the disciples are unable to stay awake and keep watch in their own emotional pain and physical fatigue.

In a similar way, it is important for us "to keep awake," and the practice of "spiritual attentiveness" helps us in this regard. It is essential to hone this discipline in a culture characterized by distraction and entertainment. Too quickly we slip into the role of spectator and fail to recognize the moments that call for our active engagement. It is worth noting that Paul uses the word *kairos* (time of opportunity) and not *chronos* (clock time) when he encourages us "to pray in the spirit at all times" (6:18). His appeal invites us to live with an attentive mind and not sleepwalk through the day's interactions. What are the times of opportunity (*kairos*) that rise up in real time (*chronos*) and become occasions for service in God's kingdom? Helmut Thielicke alludes to the potentially elusive quality of *kairos* moments when he writes of our need to embrace stillness:

> So he came because of love, in great stillness, and you can hear and see him only if you hold your own heart completely still. You must hear the good words he spoke to the poor, the quiet people. But you cannot listen to them as you listen to the loud voices of the world, as you listen to the radio and read the headlines of a newspaper. If you are afraid of the stillness, then you must necessarily miss hearing them altogether.[5]

We do not want to miss these moments because we are preoccupied by the demands of life. We want to hear the gentle whispers of our loving Abba.

Attentiveness is a spiritual discipline which we are able to nurture, and we do so by incorporating times of listening into our daily routine. This happens as we attend to the Spirit's leading in prayer. We consciously calm and quiet our minds in silence, intentionally resisting our tendency toward frenetic mental activity. As we practice the discipline of sitting and listening in prayer we cultivate a heart attitude that is sensitive to the Spirit's leading. Monologues are rarely successful in any form of communication and it is no more effective in our conversation with our loving Abba. If we are to go

---

5. Thielicke, *Waiting Father*, 50.

deeper with God it is essential that we are not always the one talking. We must provide time for listening.

Paul continues his focus on prayer as he seeks strength for heralding the "mystery of the gospel" (Eph 6:19). As we have observed, throughout his letter Paul emphasizes the theme of mystery, employing the word *mystērion* on a variety of occasions.[6] The mystery is revealed as the creation of the new humanity of God, initiated through the death and resurrection of Jesus Christ and coming to fruition through the establishment of his church, the body of Christ.[7] A significant dimension of "Christ's mystery" is found in the elusiveness of Jesus—the truth that he cannot be safely sequestered in some theological box. In his children's classic *The Lion, the Witch, and the Wardrobe*, C. S. Lewis points to this quality of wildness as Mr. Beaver and Lucy have a conversation about Aslan:

> "Then he isn't safe?" said Lucy.
>
> "Safe?" said Mr. Beaver . . . "Course he isn't safe. But he's good. He's the King, I tell you."[8]

Like Aslan, Jesus cannot be controlled by our whims and personal aspirations.

Understanding this truth, Paul seeks to be an open vessel ready to proclaim the mystery of God as presented in his Son Jesus Christ. His longing is to never hinder the gospel's message through enigmatic speech but simply be a lucid emissary who speaks the life-changing truths of the gospel of grace (Eph 6:20). To this end Paul twice requests prayer for "boldness" (6:19, 20) so that he is not curtailed by his own fears. Contemplating the challenges that he faces, he refers to himself as "an ambassador in chains" (6:20), acknowledging the pains of being shackled to a Roman soldier by heavy and restrictive chains. As Perkins notes, "Both the weight and manner of chaining prisoners made chains extremely painful. Coupled with lack of nourishment, such imprisonment could result in permanent damage to the prisoner's limbs."[9] The incarcerated apostle readily identifies his fragile, weakened state and solicits prayer so that he does not succumb to either his physical or psychological trials. We too are prone to becoming fearful in matters pertaining to security, acceptance, comfort, and health.

---

6. See Eph 3:3, 4, 5, 9; 5:32; 6:19.
7. See chapter 5, "The Spirituality of Mystery."
8. Lewis, *Lion, the Witch, and the Wardrobe*, 86.
9. Perkins, *Ephesians*, 148.

As Nouwen reminds us, "living in the house of fear" is debilitating and hinders the outward flow of love, fettering us to our egotistical concerns. With Paul, we desire the grace to stand for Jesus and to speak authentically and boldly, not constrained by "living in the house of fear" but liberated by "living in the house of love."[10]

Moving deeper into prayer draws us deeper into Christ. It is for this reason that Paul encourages his listeners to maintain open communication with the triune God. As we see elsewhere, he continually encourages the body of Christ to engage in the discipline of prayer: "Devote yourselves to prayer, keeping alert in it with thanksgiving" (Col 4:2); "Rejoice always, pray without ceasing, give thanks in all circumstances; for this is the will of God in Christ Jesus for you" (2 Thess 5:16–18); "Do not worry about anything, but in everything by prayer and supplication with thanksgiving let your requests be made known to God" (Phil 4:6). For the apostle, prayer is a mighty source of strength countering the enervating spiritual powers that attack the child of God. It acts as a force field which protects us from the enemy's pernicious ways encroaching upon our faith and trust in God. Johann Metz helps us to understand prayer's sustaining qualities:

> In the final analysis prayer is a resistance to that particular kind of hopelessness and resignation which takes root in our highly developed consciousness no matter how often we dismiss it rationally or pragmatically . . . prayer is a source of opposition, an 'intermission,' a means of resistance to that inexorable continuity which reduces us to apathy.[11]

The outcome is that prayer serves not only as defensive armor but as an offensive weapon which enables us to move into enemy territory and claim ground for the kingdom of God. In both its defensive and offensive functions, prayer is essential for the advancement of God's kingdom to align our spiritual journey with the purposes of God. It is a foundational practice which opens our minds and hearts in a spirit of humility, and provides the Spirit fertile ground for plying energizing and effective work.

---

10. Nouwen, *Lifesigns*, 16–17.
11. Rahner and Metz, *Courage to Pray*, 26–27.

Deeper into Community

Going deeper into the Divine Family requires us to do so by living dynamically within the community of faith. We have seen how Paul prays not only for the Ephesian church but desires the congregation to continuously uphold him in prayer. The bound apostle also expresses concern for the church family by sending Tychicus to report on his well-doing, elaborate on the letter's teaching, and answer any questions regarding his well-being (Eph 6:21–22).[12] Paul addresses any issues or confusion that might arise due to the challenges of long-distance communication, specifically writing that he "wants to encourage [their] hearts" by clarifying the nature of his status as a prisoner of Rome (6:22). Such a focus highlights the reality that the faith journey is never a solitary path but one that takes place within the broader body of Christ. Paul understands that his journey is not an individual effort; rather, it interconnects with all of the faith communities that he has associated with over time. Similarly, the writers of *Compassion* emphasize the communal nature of the spiritual pilgrimage as they observe,

> God's compassionate presence can never be separated from experiencing God's presence in the community to which we belong. The crises in the lives of many caring Christians today are closely connected with deep feelings of not belonging . . . [A]part from a vital relationship with a caring community a vital relationship with Christ is not possible.[13]

Lamentably, this truth is in retreat in an eroding commitment to community and a misguided faith in our own capacity for spiritual advancement. As Bonhoeffer insightfully reminds us, we have a great need for our sister's and brother's support as we pursue the sacred path:

> Therefore, the Christian needs another Christian who speaks God's word to him. He needs him again and again when he becomes uncertain and discouraged, for by himself he cannot help himself without belying the truth . . . The Christ in his own heart is weaker than the Christ in the word of his brother; his own heart is uncertain, his brother's is sure.[14]

The spiritual life is a life together and we do so by embracing it with all of its challenges and irritations and not presuming that we are able to face

---

12. See also Col 4:7–8.
13. McNeill et al., *Compassion*, 61.
14. Bonhoeffer, *Life Together*, 23.

"the rulers . . . authorities . . . and cosmic powers of this present darkness" (Eph 6:12) alone. It is imperative for us to remain in community if we want to travel deeper into Abba and hear his voice through the dynamics of living and serving together. Living apart may serve a role for a short season but it rapidly loses its effectiveness in contributing to the required dynamics for spiritual maturation.

Paul understands the church to be a blessed community, and as such it is a collective where believers grow deeper into the peace and love of Jesus Christ. This perspective is punctuated as the apostle offers a concluding benediction which summarizes the letter's key themes of peace, love, faith, and grace (6:23–24). These identified markers encapsulate the way of knowing and experiencing God's loving embrace. As we say yes to Abba's tender touch we provide space for the Holy Spirit to mold us into his creative works of art. This process of transformation occurs as we share our peace and grace with others and desire their well-being as much as our own. Isaiah speaks to this compassionate commitment as he describes the actions that God delights in: "Is not this the fast that I choose: to loose the bonds of injustice . . . to let the oppressed go free . . . to share your bread with the hungry, and bring the homeless poor into your house; when you see the naked, to cover them, and not to hide yourself from your own kin" (Isa 58:6–7). Following this supplication, the prophet cites a blessing for those who promote such a compassionate lifestyle: "Then your light shall break forth like the dawn, and your healing shall spring up quickly . . . then you shall call, and the Lord will answer; you shall cry for help, and he will say, Here I am" (58:8–9).

As we engage the blessed community by participating in God's new humanity, we incarnate the presence of his goodness within our own contexts. By experiencing and sharing Abba's love we become companions with those who are sojourning amidst the difficulties of life. As we do so, consolation is offered to those who are hurting, and the solicitude of God is made evident through our compassionate presence.

Deeper into Love

Throughout his letter Paul reminds the faith community that they are passionately loved by Jesus, and that in return they are invited to love him as his passionate bride. The apostle of Christ pursues this theme until the very end, closing his benediction with a final encouragement, "Grace be with all who have an undying love for our Lord Jesus Christ" (Eph 6:24). Translators struggle to capture the best sense of *aphtharsia*, or "undying," offering a variety of options—"incorruptible," "immortal," "sincere," "eternal life," "unfailing love," or "undying." (The NRSV and NIV both choose "undying love," as it fits with the overall arc of Paul's message in Ephesians.) It is indeed an immortal, endless, undying love which freely flows from one heart to another, or as the poet muses, from "deep to deep" (Ps 42:7). N. T. Wright embellishes the phrase by observing that we are to "lov[e] Jesus with an undying love in response to his dying love for us."[15] The dynamic of being in a relationship with Jesus is to be characterized by a love which is heartfelt, abundant, and fervent, or as the writer of the Song of Solomon espouses, "a love as strong as death" and a "passion as fierce as the grave" (Song 8:6). Such an all-encompassing love cannot be reduced to a mere creed, a series of rules, or a religious system. At the heart of being a Christian is a profound love for Jesus, oneself, one's neighbor, and God's creation. It is indeed a love without ends, as it enfolds everything it touches. The great marker for the Jesus story and its implications for humanity is this "undying love."

When my wife and I met years ago at Regent College and married a year later in the town of Canby, Oregon, for our honeymoon we traveled to the Oregon coast and spent a few days at the seaside town of Cannon Beach. In those days it was a quaint, picturesque town, boasting a massive strand of white sparkling sand and celebrated for a 340-foot-high sea stack known as Haystack Rock. It is a stunning vista, which makes for a memorable selfie, depending on the courageous spirit of the camera holder, as the outcrop rises out of the sea like an ancient Megalodon! After a few days we drove east with a car full of memories and a hitched trailer, across US 50 to Washington, DC, and north to Toronto, to make our home on the shores of Lake Ontario. Fast-forwarding—traversing a biblical generation—we traveled back to Cannon Beach for the first time since our original adventure. Over this time, the town had burgeoned and certainly more folk were walking the golden strand than we remembered. But the great marker of the soaring sea stack stood as an enduring monolith! This unvarying nature of Haystack Rock is an appropriate metaphor for the "undying love" Christ has for his bride. Even as the seamount stands frozen in time, so Christ's passion for his church never diminishes. It remains as radiant as Resurrection Sunday! In a similar fashion, we are invited to embrace and return Christ's passionate love, even as waves break and ebb

---

15. Wright, *Paul for Everyone*, 80.

upon the seashore, knowing that whatever changes may come, his "undying love" never wavers or wanes.

Questions for Reflection

1. One of the key ways we travel deeper in our relationship with Jesus is to engage daily in the practice of prayer. In light of this, write down in your journal the details of your prayer practice. Use the following questions to assist in your reflection: When and where do you pray? What types of prayer—intercession, adoration, silence, presence—do you use during the week? Are there areas you can adjust that will strengthen your prayer life?

2. Paul encourages us to be alert and to live with awareness as we make our spiritual journey. Since we are prone to losing our spiritual focus, a helpful practice for countering distraction is to spend time in silence, calm the mind, and ask for Abba's direction in carrying out the day's activities. Spend some time this week in this form of prayer and see if it helps you gain some measure of equanimity.

3. There is a focus today to laud the individual nature of faith and to highlight the importance of one's own spiritual journey. This perspective fails to recognize the essential role the community of faith plays in our spiritual pilgrimage. How do you engage the faith community as a significant player in your adventure with Christ? How do you participate in the community throughout the week? In what ways do you give back to those who travel with you in community?

4. We are invited to have an "undying love" for Jesus because he has an undying love for us. Indeed, the entire book of Ephesians unveils this amazing interchange of love. Write down in your journal some of the ways that you experience Jesus' undying love. Spend some time in meditation and prayer thanking and praising him for his loving overtures. Following this time of praise, write down some of the ways that you love him in return and how you demonstrate it throughout your everyday world.

Afterword

I have a distinct memory of facing two older boys who are selecting players for a schoolyard hockey game. There are about fifteen of us huddled together and one by one the group dwindles until a single boy stands alone. Finally, he too is waved over, and soon after the match begins. It is a vivid recollection for me, because I am the last boy chosen! My name was never called—just a slight wave of the hand acknowledged my existence—last of the bunch to be chosen for a local hockey match. I am sure such memories are commonplace enough, for we all know the disappointment of not being called first and suffering the ignominy of being taken last. Somewhere in our journey other names are heralded before ours and what we eventually experience is a casual wave, a glance of the eye, or a disinterested grunt.

As we have seen, our experience with God is the polar opposite. Our loving Father calls us into existence so that we might know the resplendent blessings of becoming his child. It is not a celestial competition. We are not standing in line under the scrutiny of the Divine Chooser. Rather, each of us is called by the Creator of the universe to achieve our specific calling for both our fulfillment and the greater good of God's kingdom. The best thing we can ever do is say yes to the limitless love of God, which is offered to us in Jesus Christ. If we do this, all other blessings are a bonus! As we draw God's love in we are able to breathe it out so that it flows over everyone we come across. Becky Hammon, an assistant coach for the San Antonio Spurs, models this type of God-inspired breathing as she talks about her relationship with God in an interview with *The New Yorker* magazine:

> She told me that Christianity gave her "courage and comfort," a sense that there was a purpose to her life. "You can't separate the two," she said, of her faith and basketball, as we sat in the kitchen of the Spurs' training facility, in San Antonio. "It would be like

AFTERWORD

trying to strain my white blood cells from my red blood cells. It would be like trying to separate my personality from my soul."[1]

For Hammon, her all-embracing vocation is clear as she breathes Jesus in and out—whether it is coaching NBA players, making chocolate-chip cookies, or attending church on Sundays. Similarly, it is this foundational calling that is meant to ground us during life's storms, comfort us in perilous times, and give us purpose amidst everyday challenges.

If our experience is self-contained, we might ask if the whole idea is a figment of our imagination—are we aligning ourselves with an unconscious desire for the infinite which finds solace in an imagined relationship with a loving God? What helps us here is an awareness that our calling is not only personal, but we participate in a collective pilgrimage. We are part of the *laos* of God—a great people comprised of individuals from every corner of the globe, from every culture and language, all joining together in the praise of our waiting Father. Moreover, the new society becomes a tangible community as we participate in the *ecclesia* situated in our own neighborhood. The community of faith that we embrace becomes the immediate gathering of saints. There our journey into love is mined, forged, and crystallized. It is in this place with all of its joys and challenges that we become our true selves. We develop the courage to let go of our false selves, which focus solely on the edification of our egos.

Unfortunately, it is this very place of transformation that we often find most difficult and shy away from because we find the journey too difficult! We naturally prefer the comfortable saunter of our own speed and selective preferences as opposed to the messy pool of conflicting opinions from other Christians whom we find disagreeable. Mysteriously, it is the morass which we find so off-putting that becomes the stuff for something extraordinary. The invitation is to enter the world of faith, where spiritual growth occurs in ways and places that transcend our limited understanding of what we think is best for the people of God. We need a vigorous commitment to enter the fray where, ironically, the beauty of God's kingdom is revealed.

To this end Paul calls the church to be the passionate bride of Christ and to do so with the enthusiasm of a dynamic symphony rather than the dreariness of a monotonous drone. His encouragement is to enter the community of faith with a full measure of joy, knowing that it is through the church that the creative musings of God are fired and eternal turns for Reality are fashioned. Of course, the focus is initially upon our own faith

---

1. Thomas, "Game Plan," 30–37.

journey, as we must let our light shine if we are to become beacons for the kingdom. Lamentably, we often resemble, as Michael Griffiths points out, "sleeping beauty," who dreams her life away, rather than keeping watch with Jesus for opportunities to proclaim the good news of the gospel.[2] We occupy ourselves with secondary concerns and lose sight of the "one thing that matters," as Kierkegaard so aptly reminds us.[3] When the body of Christ awakens from its slumber and plays its true part in the drama of God we see amazing advances for the kingdom. It is like the farmer sowing seed, with some falling on hard ground and bearing no fruit; other seed falls on rich soil bearing a harvest a hundredfold—an increase of ten thousand percent! It is this type of plentiful yield that the Father generates as his children live with passion, purpose, and imagination.

Our calling becomes transformative as we allow the mores of the good news to completely mold our lives. Doing so we become sources of light as we work out our mandate as God's daughters and sons on planet Earth. Such a lifestyle is manifested through actions of compassion as we imitate the kindness of our triune God. No longer are we self-centered, in a constant pursuit of our own comfort and satisfaction. Rather, we long for everyone to experience the boundless mercies of God. The essence of this reconstruction process takes place by planting seeds of love that bring barriers down and lift people up.

A striking example of this path of love is found in the film *Three Billboards Outside Ebbing, Missouri*, where Chief Bill Willoughby challenges his deputy Jason Dixon regarding his racist and hateful attitudes. Knowing that he is dying from cancer, Chief Willoughby leaves Jason a letter that he hopes will motivate him to embrace a lifestyle of peace. In the letter Willoughby counsels Jason that his angry spirit is hindering his development of becoming a successful police officer. Empathy is required if he is ever going to fulfill his career aspirations of becoming a skillful detective. Receiving Willoughby's counsel, Jason embarks upon a road which replaces hostility with charity, beginning with Mildred, whom he has previously considered an enemy. Chief Willoughby recognizes that the way forward is found in love's ability to transform even the hardest of hearts and it is exactly this passageway that Jason is invited to explore.

It is this same road that we are all invited to travel, as we say yes to our fundamental calling, open our hearts to Abba's life-changing love, and

2. Griffiths, *Shaking the Sleeping*.
3. Kierkegaard, *Purity of Heart*.

commit ourselves to a lifelong friendship with Jesus. As we do so together we become a magnetic field drawing people to the mercies of God and to the restorative powers made available through the body of Christ. The wounded are made well, the aimless receive purpose, the discouraged are heartened, the weak are strengthened, the lonely find comfort, and the spiritless regain fervor. As the passionate bride of Christ, in intimate relationship through his empowering presence, we become instruments of *shalom* for God's eternal glory.

Bibliography

Abraham, K. C. "A Theological Response to the Ecological Crisis." In *Theology: Voices from South and North*, edited by David G. Hallman, 65–78. Maryknoll, NY: Orbis, 1994.
Alexander, Eben. *Proof of Heaven: A Neurosurgeon's Journey into the Afterlife*. New York: Simon and Schuster, 2012.
Arends, Carolyn. "Artful Discipleship." *Faith Today*, July/August 2016, 28–31.
Avison, Margaret. *Always Now*. Vol. 1. Erin, ON: Porcupine's Quill, 2003.
Barclay, William. *The Letter to the Galatians and the Ephesians*. Rev. ed. Philadelphia: Westminster, 1976.
Barth, Markus. *Ephesians: A New Translation with Introduction and Commentary*. Vol. 2. New York: Doubleday, 1974.
Bassler, Jouette M. *Navigating Paul: An Introduction to Key Theological Concepts*. Louisville: Westminster John Knox, 2007.
Biblia de Jerusalén Latino Americana. Bilbao, Spain: Desclée de Brouwer, 2001.
Bondi, Roberta. *To Love as God Loves: Conversations with the Early Church*. Philadelphia: Fortress. 1987.
———. *To Pray and Love: Conversations on Prayer with the Early Church*. Minneapolis: Fortress, 1991.
Bonhoeffer, *Life Together*. Translated by John W. Doberstein. New York: Harper and Row, 1954.
Boring, M. Eugene. *Revelation*. Interpretation. Louisville: John Knox, 1989.
Breemen, Peter G., van. *Called by Name*. Denville, NJ: Dimension, 1976.
———. *The God Who Won't Let Go*. Notre Dame, IN: Ave Maria, 2001.
———. *Let All God's Glory Through*. New York: Paulist, 1995.
Brueggemann, Walter. *Isaiah 40–66*. Westminster Bible Companion. Louisville: Westminster John Knox, 1998.
———. *The Message of the Psalms*. Minneapolis: Augsburg, 1984.
Buechner, Frederick. *Wishful Thinking: A Theological ABC*. New York: Harper and Row, 1973.
Bunyan, John. *The Pilgrim's Progress*. Oxford: Oxford University Press, 2003.
Cahill, Thomas. *How the Irish Saved Civilization*. New York: Anchor, 1995.
Capon, Robert. *Kingdom, Grace, Judgment: Paradox, Outrage, and Vindication in the Parables of Jesus*. Grand Rapids: Eerdmans, 2002.
Cervantes, Miguel de. *Don Quixote*. Translated by Charles Jarvis. Oxford: Oxford University Press, 1998.
Chesterton, Gilbert K. *Orthodoxy: The Romance of Faith*. New York: Doubleday, 1990.

BIBLIOGRAPHY

Cousar, Charles B. *The Letters of Paul*. Nashville: Abingdon, 1996.
Cross, F. L., editor. *Oxford Dictionary of the Christian Church*. Rev. ed. Oxford: Oxford University Press, 2005.
Davey, Alan, and Elizabeth Davey. *Abba's Whisper: Listening for the Voice of God*. Eugene, OR: Wipf and Stock, 2017.
———. *Climbing the Spiritual Mountain: The Questions of Jesus*. Eugene, OR: Wipf and Stock, 2014.
Dawn, Marva. *Unfettered Hope: A Call to Faithful Living in an Affluent Society*. Louisville: Westminster John Knox, 2003.
Day, Dorothy. *The Long Loneliness*. New York: HarperCollins, 1980.
———. *Selected Writings*. Edited by Robert Ellsberg. Maryknoll, NY: Orbis, 1992.
Densham, Pen, director. *Moll Flanders*. Based on *Moll Flanders* by Daniel Defoe. Produced by John Watson et al. Trilogy Entertainment, 1996.
De Waal, Esther. *The Celtic Way of Prayer*. New York: Doubleday, 1997.
DeWitt, Calvin B., editor. *The Environment and the Christian: What Can We Learn from the New Testament?* Grand Rapids: Baker, 1991.
Dillard, Annie. *For the Time Being*. Toronto: Penguin, 1999.
Donelson, Lewis. *Colossians, Ephesians, 1 and 2 Timothy, and Titus*. Westminster Bible Companion. Louisville: Westminster John Knox, 1996.
Evans, Mary J. *Woman in the Bible*. Downers Grove, IL: InterVarsity, 1983.
Farrell, Edward. *Beams of Prayer: Spiritual Reflections with Edward J. Farrell*. Edited by Lynn Salata. New York: Alba, 1999.
———. *Surprised by the Spirit*. Denville, NJ: Dimension, 1973.
Fox, Matthew. *On Becoming a Musical Mystical Bear: Spirituality American Style*. Mahwah, NJ: Paulist, 1976.
Frankl, Viktor. *Man's Search for Meaning: An Introduction to Logotherapy*. New York: Pocket Books, 1963.
Franzoni, David, et al. *Gladiator*. Directed by Ridley Scott. Produced by Douglas Wick et al. Scott Free, 2000.
Fromm, Erich. *The Heart of Man: Its Genius for Good and Evil*. New York: Harper and Row, 1964.
Gateway Films. *Henri Nouwen*. Christian Catalyst Collection. Vision Video, 1996.
Green, Michael. "Partners in the Fellowship." In *New Testament Spirituality*, edited by Michael Green and R. Paul Stevens, 76–90. Guildford, Surrey: Eagle, 1994.
Griffiths, Michael. *Shaking the Sleeping Beauty*. Leicester, UK: Inter-Varsity, 1980.
Guiness, Oz. *The Call*. Nashville: Word, 1998.
Gutiérrez, Gustavo. *On Job: God Talk and the Suffering of the Innocent*. Translated by Matthew J. O'Connell. Maryknoll, NY: Orbis, 1987.
Hibbert, Guy. *A United Kingdom*. Based on *Colour Bar* by Susan Williams. Directed by Amma Asante. Produced by David Oyelowo et al. BBC, 2016.
Hopkins, Gerard Manley. "God's Grandeur." In *The Norton Anthology of English Literature: The Major Authors*, edited by M. H. Abrams and Stephen Greenblatt, 2158. 7th ed. New York: Norton, 2001.
Huff, Tim. *Bent Hope*. Pickering, ON: Castle Quay, 2008.
Julian of Norwich. *Revelations of Divine Love*. Translated by M. L. del Mastro. Garden City, NY: Image, 1977.
Keating, Thomas. *Foundations for Centering Prayer and the Christian Contemplative Life*. New York: Continuum, 2009.

BIBLIOGRAPHY

Kierkegaard, Søren. *Purity of Heart Is to Will One Thing: Spiritual Preparation for the Office of Confession*. Translated by Douglas V. Steere. New York: Harper and Row, 1956.

King, Martin Luther King, Jr. *The Words of Martin Luther King Jr*. Edited by Coretta Scott King. New York: Newmarket, 1996.

King, Robert, *Thomas Merton and Thich Nhat Hanh: Engaged Spirituality in an Age of Globalization*. New York: Continuum, 2003.

Kubo, Sakae. *A Reader's Greek-English Lexicon of the New Testament*. Grand Rapids: Zondervan, 1976.

Lewis, C. S. *The Four Loves*. Glasgow: William Collins, 1960.

———. *The Great Divorce*. New York: HarperCollins, 1997.

———. *The Lion, the Witch, and the Wardrobe*. New York: HarperCollins, 1978.

———. *Mere Christianity*. New York: HarperCollins, 2001.

———. "On Three Ways of Writing for Children." In *Of Other Worlds: Essays and Stories*, edited by Walter Hooper, 22–34. San Diego: Harcourt Brace Jovanovich, 1966.

———. *Reflections on the Psalms*. London: Collins, 1974.

———. *The Screwtape Letters*. New York: HarperCollins, 1998.

Lovelace, Richard F. *Renewal as a Way of Life: A Guidebook for Spiritual Growth*. Downers Grove, IL: InterVarsity, 1985.

Martin, Ralph P. *Ephesians, Colossians, and Philemon*. Interpretation. Atlanta: John Knox, 1991.

May, Gerald. *Addiction and Grace: Love and Spirituality in the Healing of Addictions*. San Francisco: HarperSanFrancisco, 1988.

———. *The Awakened Heart: Opening Yourself to the Love You Need*. San Francisco: HarperCollins, 1991.

McDonough, Martin, director. *Three Billboards Outside Ebbing, Missouri*. Produced by Graham Broadbent et al. Fox Searchlight, 2017.

McDonagh, Sean. *The Greening of the Church*. Maryknoll, NY: Orbis, 1990.

McNeill, Donald, et al. *Compassion: A Reflection on the Christian Life*. Garden City, NY: Doubleday, 1982.

Menninger, Karl. *Whatever Became of Sin?* New York: Bantam, 1973.

Merton, Thomas. *New Seeds of Contemplation*. New York: New Directions, 1961.

Mother Teresa. *A Simple Path*. Compiled by Lucinda Vardey. New York: Ballantine, 1995.

Mourneau, Robert. *Fathoming Bethlehem: Advent Meditations*. New York: Crossroad, 1997.

Moule, H. C. G. *Ephesian Studies*. Fort Washington, PA: Christian Literature Crusade, 1975.

Muddiman, John. *The Epistle to the Ephesians*. Black's New Testament Commentaries. London: Continuum, 2001.

Murray, Andrew. *With Christ in the School of Prayer*. Springdale, PA: Whitaker House, 1981.

Nhat Hanh, Thich. *Peace Is Every Breath*. New York: HarperCollins, 2011.

Nouwen, Henri. *Lifesigns: Intimacy, Fecundity and Ecstasy in Christian Perspective*. Garden City, NY: Doubleday, 1986.

———. *Our Greatest Gift: A Meditation on Dying and Caring*. San Francisco: HarperSanFrancisco, 1994.

———. *With Open Hands*. New York: Ballantine, 1985.

Obama, Barak, President. Farewell Address, January 11, 2017. http://www.cnn.com.2017/01/10.politics.

O'Keeffe, Georgia. Exhibition at the Art Gallery of Ontario, Summer 2017.

Otto, Rudolf. *The Idea of the Holy*. Translated by John Harvey. New York: Oxford University Press, 1958.

Palmer, Earl F. *Integrity: A Commentary on the Book of Philippians*. Vancouver, BC: Regent College Publishing, 1992.

Palmer, Parker J. *The Active Life: Wisdom for Work, Creativity, and Caring*. San Francisco: HarperSanFrancisco, 1990.

———. *Let Your Life Speak: Listening for the Voice of Vocation*. San Francisco: Jossey-Bass, 2000.

Peck, M. Scott. *A World Waiting to Be Born: Civility Rediscovered*. New York: Bantam, 1993.

Perkins, Pheme. *Ephesians*. Abingdon New Testament Commentaries. Nashville: Abingdon, 1997.

Peterson, Eugene H. *The Message: New Testament with Psalms and Proverbs*. Colorado Springs: NavPress, 1995.

———. *Reversed Thunder: The Revelation of John and the Praying Imagination*. San Francisco: HarperSanFrancisco, 1988.

Pinnock, Clark. *Grace Unlimited*. Bloomington, MN: Bethany Fellowship, 1975.

Postema, Don. *Space for God: Study and Practice of Spirituality and Prayer*. Grand Rapids: CRC, 1997.

Rahner, Karl. *Encounters with Silence*. Translated by James M. Demske. Westminster, MD: Christian Classics, 1.

———. *The Great Church Year: The Best of Karl Rahner's Homilies, Sermons, and Meditations*. Edited by Albert Raffelt and Harvey D. Egan. New York: Crossroad, 1995.

———. *The Practice of Christian Faith: A Handbook of Contemporary Spirituality*. Edited by Karl Lehmann and Albert Raffelt. New York: Crossroad, 1992.

Rahner, Karl, and Johann Metz. *The Courage to Pray*. London: Burns and Oates, 1980.

Rilke, Rainer Maria. *Selected Poems of Rainer Maria Rilke*. Translated by Robert Bly. New York: HarperCollins, 1981.

Roderick, Philip. *Beloved: Henri Nouwen in Conversation*. Toronto: Novalis, 2007.

Saint-Exupéry, Antoine de. *The Little Prince*. Translated by Katherine Woods. San Diego: Harcourt Brace, 1943.

Scanzoni, Letha, and Nancy Hardesty. *All We're Meant to Be*. Waco, TX: Word, 1975.

Sheldrake, Philip. *Befriending Our Desires*. Ottawa, ON: Novalis, 2001.

Shelley, Mary. *Frankenstein*. Edited by Johanna M. Smith. 3rd ed. Boston: Bedford/St. Martin's, 2016.

Simpson, E. K., and F. F. Bruce. *The Epistles to the Ephesians and Colossians*. New International Commentary on the New Testament. Grand Rapids: Eerdmans, 1957.

Smith, Raymond. "The Virtue of Docility." *The Thomist* 15:4 (October 1952) 572–623.

Snyder, Howard A. *The Community of the King*. Downers Grove, IL: InterVarsity, 1977.

Stott, *God's New Society: The Message of Ephesians*. Downers Grove, IL: InterVarsity, 1979.

Talbert, Charles H. *Ephesians and Colossians*. Grand Rapids: Baker Academic, 2007.

Taylor, Daniel. *The Myth of Certainty: Trusting God, Asking Questions, Taking Risks*. Grand Rapids: Zondervan, 1992.

Teilhard de Chardin, Pierre. *The Phenomenon of Man*. Translated by Bernard Wall. New York: Harper and Row, 1975.

———. *Toward the Future*. Translated by René Hague. San Diego: Harcourt Brace Jovanovich, 1975.
Thielicke, Helmut. *The Waiting Father: Sermons on the Parables of Jesus*. Harper and Row, 1957.
Thiselton, Anthony. *The Living Paul: An Introduction to the Apostle's Life and Thought*. Downers Grove, IL: InterVarsity, 2009.
Thomas, Louisa. "Game Plan." *The New Yorker*, April 16, 2018, 30–37.
Thompson, Francis. "The Hound of Heaven." In *The Country of the Risen King: An Anthology of Christian Poetry*, compiled by Merle Meeter. Grand Rapids: Baker, 1978.
Underhill, Evelyn. *An Anthology of the Love of God*. Edited by Lumsden Barkway and Lucy Menzies. London: Mowbrays, 1976.
———. *Concerning the Inner Life*. Oxford: Oneworld, 1995.
———. *The Spiritual Life*. London: Hodder and Stoughton 1996.
Vanier, Jean. *Community and Growth*. London: Darton, Longman and Todd, 1990.
Van Rossum, Mary Lou. *Reinhabiting the Earth: Biblical Perspectives and Eco-Spiritual Reflections*. Liguori, MO: Triumph, 1994.
Walsh, Fran, et. al. *The Lord of the Rings: The Fellowship of the Rings*. Based on *The The Lord of the Rings: The Fellowship of the Ring*s by J. R. R. Tolkien. Directed by Peter Jackson. Produced by Barrie M. Osborne et al. WingNut Films, 2001.
Walsh, James, editor. *The Cloud of Unknowing*. Mahwah, NJ: Paulist, 1981.
Waltke, Bruce K. *Finding the Will of God: A Pagan Notion?* 2nd ed. Grand Rapids: Eerdmans, 2016.
Ware, James P, editor. *Synopsis of the Pauline Letters in Greek and English*. Grand Rapids: Baker Academic, 2010.
Webber, Robert. *Planning Blended Worship: The Creative Mixture of Old and New*. Nashville: Abingdon, 1998.
———. *Worship Is a Verb*. Waco, TX: Word, 1985.
Westermann, Claus. *Praise and Lament in the Psalms*. Atlanta: John Knox, 1981.
Wilson, August. *Fences*. New York: Penguin, 1986.
Wood, A. Skevington. "Ephesians." In *The Expositor's Bible Commentary*, vol. 11, edited by Frank E. Gaebelein, 3–92. Grand Rapids: Zondervan, 1978.
Wright, N. T. *Paul: In Fresh Perspective*. Minneapolis: Fortress, 2009.
———. *Paul for Everyone: The Prison Letters, Ephesians, Philippians, Colossians, and Philemon*. London: SPCK, 2002.
Zaillian, Steven. *Schindler's List*. Based on *Schindler's Ark* by Thomas Keneally. Produced and directed by Steven Spielberg et al. Amblin Entertainment, 1993.

www.ingramcontent.com/pod-product-compliance
Lightning Source LLC
Chambersburg PA
CBHW071232170426
43191CB00032B/1360